THOSE ENGLISH!

THOSE ENGLISH!

BY

KURT VON STUTTERHEIM

TRANSLATED BY

L. MARIE SIEVEKING

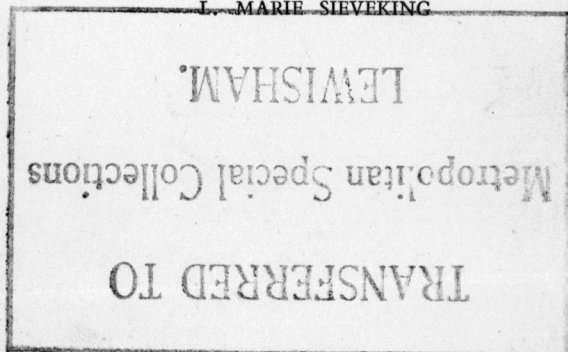

LONDON

SIDGWICK & JACKSON, LTD.

1937

PRINTED IN GREAT BRITAIN BY
WILLIAM CLOWES AND SONS, LIMITED, LONDON AND BECCLES.

PREFACE

THIS book is an attempt to fill what I believe to be a gap in the average German's knowledge of England. Many remarkable German books have been written on England's great institutions and her social organizations. It was not my intention to compete with them, and I have contented myself with a rather sketchy survey of English democracy, imperialism, religion, law, education, theatre, literature, and so on.

It may strike the English reader that I have given what he may think a disproportionate space to such matters as manners, taste, tact, humour, conventions, fashions, and to the doings of "Society." I did so, as I feel that the average German is inclined to take suburbia and what it represents for the whole of England. During my fifteen years' stay in this country I met many of my compatriots who spoke English quite well when they came to England. After a month spent in England they were unable to "walk." They "proceeded."

Had it been the other way round and had Germany known all about English country houses, the perfect beauty of old English furniture, about the ease of good English manners, and the broadmindedness of the worldly Englishman and Englishwoman, I would have written a book stressing the extreme importance of those classes who have no share in these special achievements. I would not have thought it necessary to point out that the England of the villas, the "Ye Olde Inns," and of the people who are shocked by an unclad statue, is not

v

England. I would, on the contrary, have underlined all that is to be said for the backbone of England.

But this has been done over and over again. Therefore, in bringing other aspects of English life to the limelight, I merely tried to help my compatriots to see England in what I believe to be her right proportions.

The English reader will see that I am neither an Anglomaniac nor an Anglophobe, trying only to be fair and giving more space to description than to analysis. If I do not want my countrymen to copy England, I want them to understand her. This fostering of understanding and therefore of friendship between old England and young Germany was my principal aim.

K. V. St.

CONTENTS

vii

CHAPTER I

THE ENGLISHMAN

IT is not mere chance that has caused so many books to be written about England since the end of the War. A world that has grown accustomed to storm and change finds it hard to realize that there should still exist a country in its midst that has gone peacefully on its own evolutionary way. This is not to imply that everything has remained the same in England. Far from it. There have been great changes. But it is the manner in which these changes take place, the fact that the protagonists are hardly aware that they are taking place, which forms the difference between England and the other civilizations in the world to-day.

The world is not unnaturally curious regarding a country and its people whose evolution is like that of a vegetable organism when all about them is seething. It is only one step farther to the question whether the same laws will govern the future of England as those which have held good in the past and present. The Englishman does not concern himself unduly about this problem. He trusts in his star and in the genius of his race to cope with difficulties as they arise. Only the wisest—or possibly the most foolish—occasionally wonder whether England will be as much the darling of the god of the twentieth century as it was of the gods of the eighteenth and nineteenth centuries.

Once the English had finished with the unfortunate Stuarts, everything was easy. The State system of which the foundations were then laid proved to be the fittest for survival in modern times. At the same time a new type of man arose in response to the demands of the age. The brilliant, witty Stuart cavalier, with his tendency to drink, his poetry, debts, and love-affairs, gave place to that curious blend of chivalry and matter-of-fact bourgeoisie—the gentleman. Puritanism took terrible toll of all that makes life beautiful. But once the moral thunderstorm was over a man emerged who was exactly fitted for the tasks that awaited him and for the new social order that he was about to build up. Enough of the knightly adventurer still lived in this new English-man to enable him to conquer a world-empire. But the merchant's quill went alongside the knight's sword, and together they brought a quarter of the world under the English flag. To this very day the two trends may be seen in the English character—courage, joy in danger, and the most cold-blooded bargaining. No Englishman carries quixotry so far as to forget his cheque-book; but hardly one is too stolid to break out once in a while into a quixotic act. People with mild, sheep-like faces will suddenly elope with a pretty chorus-girl, or set out to tramp through the Gobi desert on foot.

In truth the inhabitants of this island are one of the wonders of the world. One may live in England for years, and still keep on discovering fresh facets in the singular character of its people. Indeed, it is only by living in the closest intimacy with the English that it is possible to gain any understanding of their mentality. For the Englishman hates to reveal himself; in fact it is considered bad manners to talk about oneself. Charles Morgan, the novelist, designates the capacity to convey their feelings "without parade of words" as the main characteristic of his countrymen. If the English treat one another as though they were Great Powers, they are even more stately in their dealings with foreigners, who commit such solecisms and are so embarrassing, whose ideas are so clever and whose actions so foolish, who are untrustworthy and odd, and never know what is "the thing" and what is not. Such is the attitude of a nation which, in consequence of its world-empire and its love of travelling, has had more to do with foreigners than any other. The Englishman is not happy in intercourse with foreigners. They may amuse him and he may make life-long friendships with them. But he is only at home when he is "at home." And it is only here that he reveals his true nature. Hence it is a mistake to judge the Englishman by those of his countrymen who may be met travelling abroad or who have settled in Rome or Paris. In the same way care must be taken not to draw inferences from English authors and thinkers and apply them to the average Englishman. English though intellectual England may be, it is separated by a deep gulf from the workaday Englishman, who refuses firmly to have anything to do with "highbrows." In this connection "highbrows" are to be understood as including not merely blue-stockings and daubers, but any man or woman who does not conceal his or her intellectual interests or erudition as though they were something to be apologised for. Montmartre and Schwabing were parts of the general life of a people, and Paris and Munich were proud of them. Chelsea, on the other hand, while it remained the artists' quarter, was looked upon by the man in the street as an island, the strange inhabitants of which did not really belong to England. Thus the annual Chelsea Arts' Ball, despite its brilliant setting, is a lifeless and theatrical affair.

This must not be taken to imply that the Englishman has no understanding of art and science. Exhibitions in London have to close their doors because of over-crowding; and tickets will be found to be practically unobtainable for the concerts that make the greatest possible demands on the audience. This proves how strong are the contrasts between the intellectual and the average Englishman. No greater mistake can be made than to judge England by rule of thumb. Can a people be called "cold" that forms a single pulsating mass on the night of a King's Jubilee? Can men be called "money-grubbers" who spend millions in charity? Can a nation be accused of having no ideals that was within an ace of starting a war for the sake of the League of Nations? On the other hand, where else in Europe does money form such a barrier as in England, where two sisters, one of whom marries a rich man and the other a poor one, will hardly see anything of one another? Societies for the protection of animals ensure that no member of the brute creation shall suffer harm, while an increas-ing number of charges of cruelty to children are brought in the law courts. No one will doubt the democratic sentiments of the English people. None the less, titles and class distinctions have maintained a positively mediæval value. These examples and con-tradictions, which may be multiplied at will, are only adduced to show how dangerous it is to try to reduce Englishmen to a common denominator. There is no means of understanding the English character except by a lively and unprejudiced sympathy. This is not made easier by the fact that, as Morgan says, the Englishman expresses himself in deeds instead of words, and his nature urges him to self-concealment rather than self-revelation. To plumb such a man requires above all extreme tact. Only by the application of tact may the veil that hangs before the curiously shy and sensitive soul of the Englishman be raised enough to permit of a glance beyond it.

The Englishman is the product of an old civilization. He is civilized man *par excellence*. He has left his origins so far behind that he has forgotten them. In the consciousness of the English people English history begins with Queen Elizabeth and her father's matrimonial adventures. Of the remoter past only isolated incidents, such as William the Conqueror and Magna Charta, mean anything to them. The English have no mythological memories. They know nothing of their heathen gods, nor do they feel any kind of mystic bond with their ancient forefathers. Yggdrasil and its squirrel mean nothing to them. England has no Song of the Nibelungs, no epic of Gudrun, and Beowulf, even if better known, would touch no chord. Not even King Arthur and the Arthurian legends—which in any case are of Celtic origin—have filled the gap, apart from the fact that these noble knights cannot be identified with barbarian ancestors. There are not even any ancient folk-tales that might provide a field for exploration by English brothers Grimm. The German's heart beats higher when history ends and legend begins. To the Englishman the remoter past of his nation is dead. It has been kept alive only in the hearts of the Celts, who live in Ireland, Wales, and the Scottish Highlands.

The mythological tendency of the German people is closely allied with its love of nature. In both worlds the German sees the working of eternal forces in which he longs to be merged, to become one with them. This romantic pantheistic yearning that is part of every German's make-up is alien to the Englishman—unless he chances to be a poet, such as those who have written England's great nature poetry. As far as the average Englishman is concerned, nature is an æsthetic or idyllic concept, and very often merely a playground. Nature, in his view, is less an end in itself than a potential field of action. He walks through the meadows in order to give his dog a run. He goes to a river to fish; on to the moors to shoot grouse; on to a lawn to play tennis. He loves his garden because he can grow flowers in it; his parks and trees because they make a splendid setting for his house. He loves his animals, with whom he feels a kinship greater than that with the earth to whose womb he has no desire to return. The Englishman's greatest feeling of unity is with his fellow men, while he feels himself and the earth to be two rather alien beings. Possibly the soul of this nation of seafarers is more in harmony with the perpetual motion of the sea.

Though the English feeling for nature is not so profound as that of the German, the love of nature is common to both peoples. England is full of country-houses and week-end cottages, and in the summer of tents and caravans. The amount of fresh air consumed by the Englishman, who spends every spare moment in the open, is immense. And, being physically hardy, he is able to stand conditions that would completely prevent many a foreigner from enjoying himself at all. Even in his dealings with Nature the Englishman is master and not disposed to give in to her moods. Man has emerged victorious from the long struggle. Nature in England has been tamed, the landscape has been divided up into gardens and parks that turn whole counties into green idylls. Only in Scotland and Wales and certain districts of the north of Devon and Yorkshire does Nature still make her voice heard. Southern England and the Lake District have been domesticated.

The German's pantheistic love of nature has brought about a close union in his mind between religion and nature that is foreign to an Englishman's mentality. An Englishman regards religion as a private affair between himself and God that is quite separate from any divine manifestations in the non-human creation. The one definite thing is the written and revealed word of God, the literary biblical message of the Creator to mankind. It satisfies the Englishman's metaphysical, and above all his ethical, needs. For every Englishman is a moralist, a man to whom good and bad on earth are of more moment than any search after the eternal verities. There is nothing of the Faust in his soul. He is content to accept revealed religion or he retires into agnosticism. Nevertheless, the English agnostic is not so foolish as to sink into a stolid materialism. It is significant that Hamlet's words: "There are more things in Heaven and earth, Horatio, than are dreamt of in your philosophy," should be some of the most frequently quoted lines in

English literature. The existence of supernatural beings is regarded by the Englishman as a matter of fact, even though it may only be in the guise of spiritualism and the ghosts which seem to have turned English country-houses into veritable homes for earth-bound spirits. The veil of Maya does not worry the English. But very few would deny its existence.

For many Englishmen, however, the veil has already been lifted. This is the great mass of those whose feet are firmly planted upon the floor of the Church and especially upon that of the numerous nonconformist sects. For even if the number of definite believers has fallen since the days of Queen Victoria, it nevertheless remains enormous, and the Church may still be accounted one of the strongest forces in the country. Far more often than sceptics will admit, England's faith is honest and derives from deeply religious springs. Even when this is not wholly the case, the English Church has a mighty ally in the reverence that the English nation has for tradition. And it is surely very typical of the Englishman that he has assumed his spiritual world to be a kind of State, with God as king and the bishops as His ministers. Having put nature in its place, having drawn a dividing line between himself and the mists of the past, it was only logical that the Englishman should give his Church and his religion a form that he can regard as fixed and immutable. He is thus able to turn with a quiet mind to face the great tasks to which he feels himself called. No mysterious forces lurk in the background. The Englishman has made his peace with them.

This great act of limitation is the Englishman's

strength and his weakness. It takes from him the metaphysical atmosphere that enfolds the soul of the German and the Slav. "Russia has no boundaries; Russia reaches to God," could never have been written of England. England consists of a network of limitations. England's great physicists may think in æons, its political boundaries may stretch across the world. But England's life has no link with infinity. No breath of eternity blows across the island. Wherever one may look, evidences are seen of this self-imposed limitation. Thus English life may take on a ghastly kind of matter-of-factness and aridity, which even the English themselves endeavour to avoid, seeking in other lands what they miss in their own homes.

On the other hand, the Englishman gains in stability what he loses in breadth of vision. His forces, not being dissipated, can be concentrated upon the task which he feels himself called upon to perform. And the task he has set himself is to tackle life as a whole and to provide himself with a technique of living that shall be ready for every emergency. This statement is made in the same sense as that which says that the Prussian lives for his duty, the Indian for his soul, the Japanese for his Emperor, the Mohammedan for Allah, and the hero of a German "Entwicklungsroman" for his cultural and spiritual harmony. While, however, these characteristics are dominant in the life of the above-named peoples, and indeed may be said to be their ultimate *raison d'être*, the Englishman's interests are absorbed by "every-day" matters. True, the expression "every-day" must not be taken in too circumscribed a sense. It does not refer only to business and eating and drinking, but includes everything that goes to make up a civilized and interesting life—manners and taste, friendship and love, politics, art, comfort, hospitality, and much else. The Englishman's mind may not be concentrated upon things spiritual and abstract in the manner which was the ideal of so many Germans. But neither is he a crass materialist only out to make money. He has nothing in common with the German of the era after 1870. The Englishman deals with problems as they present themselves from day to day, and does his best to settle them without offending against law and morality. But in so far as it is possible he avoids having recourse to the methods of the sergeant-major or the bureaucrat. Such means are so alien to the Englishman that Lao-tse's saying: "A great kingdom must be ruled with delicacy, as small fish are fried," might be written up over the gates of England. The Englishman believes with the Chinese sage that he best controls things who makes use of the forces inherent in them and turns them to his own advantage with care and tact. English life is built from top to bottom upon the principle that A endeavours to persuade B to do upon his own initiative whatever it is that A wants done. It is the same in Parliament and in the nursery. The Englishman abhors force because he believes that an action done under compulsion can never have the same value as a voluntary one. Hence his fundamental readiness to compromise. Only if he sees that all his blandishments are failing does the scene change. Then—always supposing that it is an affair of importance—the polite and kindly Englishman is capable of becoming in the twinkling of an eye one of the harshest people imaginable. Similarly, in international politics the Englishman is a totally different person before and after a declaration of war. This was seen during the World War, when the English propaganda far and away surpassed that of all Germany's other enemies, to say nothing of her own. The moment he begins to fight, his motto is "Force." But hardly had the victory been won than a great part of the English people ceased from hatred. The English spirit and the sound common-sense of the English demanded that a means should be found for living in peace and amity with Germany. Unfortunately for Europe this spirit took a long time to win through.

Anyone who wishes to tackle life as the Englishman does must be very sure of himself and not be subject to mental vacillations. Hence English education is primarily an education in self-confidence, without which no one can exist on this island and which seems to be lacking in hardly any Englishman. Hence even the least ambitious and most retiring person may evince personality. In order to attain this object the Englishman makes use of two means above all others. He avoids loading his own brains, and especially those of his children, with more knowledge than is compatible with decisiveness. He discovered early that excessive cultivation of the intellect is destructive of personality unless character acts as a counterpoise. If it is a case of either being a great man in small surroundings or chancing a hazardous leap into higher spheres, the Englishman prefers to cling to the earth. For he respects the former, whereas a very much keener but unpractical mind irritates him. While the Englishman will overlook many weaknesses, he is merciless to indecision. A lack of firmness appears to him undignified. In the same way that the Englishman encourages mental curiosity only with great reserve, so—and this is his second educational means—he is opposed to unnecessary experiments. The Englishman does not make it easy for himself to find a form—or a new form—for things old or new. He works slowly, like Nature. But once the form exists, whether it is a law or a custom or simply a social convention, the Englishman does not care to have it tampered with. The Englishman is sparing with the axe because he lets things grow like a tree. This explains the curious preference of this individualistic people for the standard which sometimes makes English life so monotonous and which nevertheless saves the individual so much labour. The method of laying a table, of laying out a flower-bed, which room should be used as a bedroom and which as the dining-room, what sort of things should be eaten at lunch and what at dinner, what clothes should be worn, and much else, is all prescribed by tradition. It has become crystallized, and does not even require any particular thought. Entire sections of life have through the work of generations received a permanent form, which has only to be learnt. England is not a country, it is a habit.

To grow into the kind of person who is capable of tackling life is the Englishman's prime object. His intellect is applied intellect, not wit for wit's sake. Averse from speculation and introspection, the Englishman takes life as it comes. It is his perpetual study and is the teacher that he is prepared to recognize. In the school of life he has learnt to mistrust logic. It is only in the play of the intellect and not in life itself that anything inevitably follows upon given premisses. There is never any doubt in the Englishman's mind as to which of the two is " right." It is always life that is right—life that is in a continual state of flux and in which no one can predict what it will bring forth on the morrow. It is from this realization that one of the Englishman's fundamental postulates has arisen—never to post-date his cheques on life. "Don't cross your bridges before you come to them," is one of the proverbs of a nation that, more than almost any other, is averse from planning ahead, whether in small matters or great. It is a mistake to say that the British world-empire is the result of a vast scheme. The English themselves say: "The British Empire is an accident." And anyone who studies their history is bound to admit that this is true. Cecil Rhodes would never have caused such a stir with his Cape-to-Cairo project if men of his type were not so rare in England. Although there are occasions on which England's diplomacy is far-reaching, it much more usually follows a hand to mouth existence.

The English never understand what is meant when foreigners speak of "perfidious Albion." For they are true to themselves only while they do in January what seems right in January, just as in December they acted as seemed proper to them at that time. Consequently the foreign Chancellery that assumes from what has been done in December what *will* be done in January will do so at its own risk. It cannot complain if the sum does not work out correctly.

An immense amount of self-confidence is necessary for such a technique of life. Only a man who feels that his forces will be sufficient when the time comes can afford to take no thought for the morrow. Only such a man can rely upon being able to make a right decision at a given moment. Nevertheless, rapid as are the Englishman's decisions, determined as is his action, he would frequently fall into difficulties if he were not able to rely upon his never-failing instinct. When the Englishman broke down the bridge that carried him into civilization from his primeval forest, he kept with him this positively animal perceptiveness. It is this which distinguishes English rationalism from that of the Latin, who is much cleverer and who yet frequently stumbles where the Englishman finds his way with the security of a sleep-walker. "We muddled through," the English say of themselves after any crisis. For despite his self-confidence the Englishman is not vain. On the contrary, the natural modesty of the Englishman is one of his most pleasing characteristics.

At the same time, the Englishman's modesty is not wholly disconnected with a recognition of the fact that they who vaunt themselves shall be abased. The English are born psychologists and understand very perfectly the reactions of the human mind. They know that action and reaction are equal and opposite, just as exaggerated statements evoke contradiction. Hence understatement has become one of the rules of the game of life in England. No Englishman would say: "I made a great success" of anything. The proper means of expressing this is to say: "I don't think I did it too badly." The person to whom he is speaking will know what is meant. The English understand each other wonderfully well. A casual word suffices in cases in which other nations would overflow in long explanations. Here again it is to be noted that the same rule holds good in public as in private life. Even the Press, at all events the most responsible part of it, is given to understatement. The same is true of politics. Apart from times of war, when nothing is normal, an English politician avoids violent language, does not bang his fist upon his desk. His aim is not to bludgeon the world at home or abroad, but to win it over to his point of view, like a merchant trying to sell his goods. In the policy of a nation of shopkeepers the idea of goodwill must necessarily play a considerable part.

This brings us to the famous question of the Englishman's political talents. Every history book supplies the answer, though it would be a mistake to suppose that the English nation racks its brains about political problems. The difference between England and Germany in this matter may be observed by listening to the conversations in any small inn in the two countries. The Germans will talk as if world-policy were centred in their own village. Not so the English. Their talk will be of weather and holidays, of business, sport, and the bringing-up of children. Let these mild family men be put into an awkward situation, however, and they will get themselves out of it much more readily than their more politically-minded German brothers. The English are politicians because they act politically, not because they concern themselves with political questions. Even the English language is political with its "woulds" and "mights," its vagueness of expression that always leaves room for compromise, and its frequent use of the word "suggest." Even the English voice that is never raised, the English eye that never blazes, the apparently gentle abstraction, are not wanting in political effect. Even

English politeness, kindly as the Englishman may be by nature, has a diplomatic tone.

When an Englishman tries to imagine what is most likely to impress the stranger within his gates, he flatters himself that it is his individualism. In fact the foreigner wherever he looks sees standards and clichés and conventions, and is apt to be somewhat disappointed. On the other hand, he is in a perpetual state of wonder at English politeness, which is found in all classes and which survives tests that would lead to swearing and personalities on the Continent. London is incomparably more polite as a city than Paris. Its courtesy is far more sincere than that of Rome and much more natural than the somewhat regimented politeness of Berlin. There is reason in English courtesy, moreover, and its use is confined to reasonable occasions, instead of being expressed in senseless gestures, in bowings, in introductions, in hand-shaking. Instead of all this, an Englishman seeing a stranger looking at the numbers on the houses will ask: "Can I direct you?" And time and again cars will pull up to offer a lift to an unknown pedestrian who looks tired. If ever an Englishman can lend a helping hand without putting himself to too great trouble he is always ready to do so. This everyday courtesy is perhaps the purest expression of English kindliness and as such ranks higher than mere convention.

Courtesy is also useful as a means of government, and conduces towards good relations between persons. Many things have been settled merely by courtesy in England that might otherwise have led to serious crises. Compromise is one of the Englishman's chief aims, and he avoids as far as possible rousing sharp antagonisms. The fact that differences of opinion seldom give rise to violent conflict, and in consequence that English life even now runs as if on springs, is not to be attributed solely to good psychology and the general habit of courtesy. One of the most important means of relieving tension in England is the English sense of humour.

If human attributes may be divided into primary and secondary, humour is certainly among the former in England. Humour in this country is not a mere matter of laughter or witticisms. In England it has been raised to the dignity of a philosophy. Humour is the Englishman's fundamental attitude to life, and because it is a part of his nature he never loses it. The Englishman's profoundest wisdom lies in his sense of humour that prevents him from taking things too seriously and thus losing the slight detachment that makes life easier to control. Humour is, moreover, the great corrective medicine with which the Englishman doses himself. No individual and, taken all in all, no nation laughs and smiles at itself as much as these islanders do. It follows that a man who has no sense of humour has a bad time of it. Among the defects that the naturally lenient Englishman cannot forgive, bad manners and the lack of a sense of humour take first place. No one who cannot laugh is taken seriously in England. He cannot enjoy full rights of citizenship in a community that looks up to humour as to a god—or an idol. Humour may indeed become an idol if it prevents its disciples from penetrating those regions into which its dominion cannot extend. The bad side of this dictatorship of humour is shown in a certain tendency to superficiality in the

English character, in the habit of clever men of avoiding serious conversation, in the reputation enjoyed by shallow persons purely for the sake of their power to evoke laughter, in the capacity of humour to mask moral ineptitude or actually to paralyse mental energy. Nevertheless, the blessings of humour are out of all proportion greater. It is to humour that England owes many of the pearls of its literature and wisdom, to humour that it owes its inborn philosophy of life, many of the charms of existence and social intercourse, and not least a lessening of class-distinctions.

It would be impossible for humour, however kindly, to play this part in English life were it not that in his heart of hearts the Englishman is an incurable optimist. Millions of Englishmen, it is true, live in conditions that are unfit for human beings. But the nation as such has been more fortunate than any other nation in the world. A long history has taught the English to trust in their star. Thus few Englishmen are ever despondent; there are few who despite set-backs are not always ready to make a fresh start. A tragic attitude to life, such as is found in Germany, is just as alien to the Englishman as Slav pessimism. In cases where the Russian would say resignedly "Nietchevo!" and the German would see the inevitable workings of fate, the Englishman exclaims: "Cheer up! Have another shot at it!" Even if he does not succeed in the end, the Englishman does not curse God and man. He recognizes his own incapacity, metaphorically speaking shrugs his shoulders, and admits without envy that others are luckier or cleverer than himself. As a result of this lack of jealousy in the English character luxurious motor cars may be driven through the worst slums without rousing any hostility. It seems as though, on the contrary, the poorest among the poor enjoyed the reflected glory of those who are more fortunate than themselves. A systematic political propaganda was necessary to awaken the feeling of social injustice among the poorer strata in this land of gross inequalities. The English were obliged to learn in a political classroom something that comes natural to the French. There they forgot their ancient wisdom that each man forges his own destiny.

The British Isles have thus produced a type that has created its own limitations. But within these limits—and they are very wide—the Englishman demands full sovereignty. He no more permits his own temperament to run away with him than he does external circumstances. Self-discipline and self-control have become as much a part of his flesh and blood as his innumerable conventions. They form the counterpoise to English individualism. Even this latter, however, does not mean that each man is determined to be his own poet, philosopher, and guide. Its expression takes the form of a very clearly-defined independence. "Don't interfere" and "Mind your own business" are among the foremost rules of English life. "Don't poke your nose into things that don't concern you!" But reserve is not the same as unsociableness. The Englishman is a most sociable creature. He may live in a lonely house, but so far as his means permit he will fill it with guests. He enjoys increasing his own sense of well-being by that of his fellows. Kind-hearted by nature, he likes to give pleasure to other people. His readiness to give a helping

hand has not its equal in Europe. He is "easy-going"—
that is to say, once he has overcome his natural reserve
and has made friends with anyone, he omits superfluous
formalities. In small things and great he prefers a light
hand. He would rather stay on the surface of things and
preserve harmony than penetrate into profundities and
risk dispute. People do not quarrel, they agree to
differ. If, however, it becomes necessary to deliver a
rebuke, then it is done firmly and frankly, like a storm
that clears the air. This seldom occurs. People understand each other so well that if their natures are anti-
pathetic they simply keep out of each other's way. It
must be admitted, however, that what English life gains
in peaceableness it loses in interest. The English can be
indescribably dull, and are capable of demonstrating a
lack of alertness that makes any conversation, apart from
weather and sport, impossible. Whole classes of society
suffer not merely from mental indolence but from an
actual hostility to intellect that has condemned many of
the great minds of this country to isolation.

Not that the Englishman is lacking in intellectual
gifts. He himself makes a distinction between two kinds
of intelligence—brilliance and sound judgment. While
clever and witty people are rarer in England than in
France, there is a great number of those who can boast
of an excellent critical faculty and a sound common
sense. The Englishman is pre-eminent in his capacity
to take a rapid and comprehensive view of a complicated
situation, to say nothing of his ability for judging men.
Scientific psychology may have been carried to greater
heights in other countries, but in England the whole of
life is a vast laboratory for applied psychology. The very

fact that the Englishman objects as far as possible to forcing people to do anything means that he is obliged to consider their psychic reactions.

Finally, the individual's relationship to the State is peculiar in England. Patriotic as is the average Englishman, he only renders to Cæsar that which is Cæsar's, and watches jealously to see that the State shall not interfere in his private sphere. Thus Englishmen are not easy to organize, except voluntarily, and even then only in small groups. It is exceptionally difficult to induce the English people to agree to great compulsory organizations of an economic or political nature. Wherever possible the Englishman relies upon himself or upon the self-organization of life. The world of to-day, where the *laisser faire* attitude will no longer solve problems, exposes this system to severe tests. In the past it helped to awaken in the Englishman, who did not rely upon the help of the government, a strong sense of responsibility for his own weal and woe and for the well-being of his fellow citizens. Thus the best Englishmen combine a sense of responsibility and public spirit with the sturdy independence of their race. It is men of this type, men who are capable of working with the same energy both for themselves and for the commonwealth, who have made England great.

CHAPTER II

THE ENGLISHWOMAN

THE time is long past when the Suffragette movement caused England to rock as in the throes of
revolution. Women are in possession of the hotly
disputed vote, and Mrs. Pankhurst has been raised from a
prison cell on to a pedestal. The House of Commons,
nevertheless, contains very few female members, and
despite excellent individual achievements, women have
not come to the forefront in parliamentary life. Nevertheless, the Suffragette movement remains a social
landmark of the greatest importance, since it brought to
a successful conclusion the Englishwoman's long
struggle to have equal rights with men. Nowadays
equality of rights is taken so much as a matter of course
that no one wastes a word on the subject.

American women, it is true, do not admit that this is
the case. They treat their menfolk as Oriental men treat
their women, and still regard England as a country
where men are supreme. A comparison must be made
with continental Europe in order to understand the
situation which the Englishwoman has created for
herself within her own family as well as in public life.
One of her most valuable allies in the struggle was
the Englishman's cherished cult of independence.
Generations of men made a religion of their independence and it was inevitable that one day women

should demand to pray in the same temple. At the turn of the century the position of the tyrannical father and husband—a not infrequent phenomenon in Victorian England—was shattered. Since then wives and daughters have come progressively more to the front. The World War and the subsequent economic difficulties that necessitated women's entering the labour market proved here as everywhere else to be a help towards the emancipation of women. The World War in which millions of men gave their lives on the various fronts ended in a victory for woman.

The Englishman did not feel altogether happy during the period of transition. His natural chivalry bade him look after women and forbade him to deny them anything—and the harder the former grew to be for him the more difficult he found the latter. Moreover, the women and girls of this generation developed a boundless energy, while the men only too frequently held to their old traditions of easy-going and *laisser aller*. Thus the men were simply swept away by the rush of feminine activity. Before they knew where they were, Miss X had her own latchkey and Mrs. Y claimed the right to go to Paris whenever she felt like it. At the same time a considerable section of cultural and social initiative was transferred to feminine hands. Women suddenly proved themselves to be mentally more alert than men, who felt that they had done all that could be expected of them when they had passed a certain number of hours at work in the City. Women, on the other hand, found time to attend to intellectual matters in addition to their domestic and social affairs. Had it not been for women, London would never have won its present position in the world of music. Art exhibitions are full of women's work, and feminine names are frequently to be found in the catalogues of publishing houses. The country that gave birth to Jane Austen and the Brontë sisters in the past has proved once again to be a fruitful soil for feminine literary and journalistic gifts. Naturally the percentage of mediocrity is considerable, but names like Virginia Woolf and Katherine Mansfield prove that women have no cause to be ashamed of their contribution to modern literature. And the two names of Laura Knight and Dod Procter suffice to show that the same is true of painting.

Even greater has been the number of women who have felt impelled to practical work. Financial gifts like Lady Rhondda's are rare, although there are plenty of women who are excellent at managing their property. On the other hand, women discovered a fruitful sphere of action in the field of social welfare. In all forms of welfare organization women have frequently proved to be the motive power. In the same way they have done excellent work in municipal administration. English women are not only dowered with initiative and admirable moral courage, they also show remarkable powers of persuasive speech. This explains the part played by women at political meetings and in the organization of all Parties. Even the most anti-feminist die-hard will not refuse the help of women as house-to-house canvassers. Many a Member of Parliament owes his seat to the canvassing powers of his wife and daughters, who are equally enthusiastic whether they are Conservative aristocrats or revolutionary Radicals. The number is legion, too, of women working for temperance, for the protection of animals, for pacifism, and for the League of Nations.

In view of the wide ramifications of public activities, the question naturally arises as to what is left over for family life; what kind of wife and mother the English-woman makes. It is certainly true to say that she goes her own way, and that it never dawns on her to be sub-missive to her husband or to regard his word as law. The woman who is a slave to her husband hardly exists nowadays in England, where not only men but also women have their own banking accounts. On the other hand, the domestic tyrant is also rare. For marriages are contracted on the tacit understanding that each partner shall have his own sphere in which the other does not interfere. Certain reserves are main-tained even in marriage, not only between husband and wife but also between parents and children. Suggestion is preferred to command and disputes are avoided in private life as in public.

Despite participation in public affairs, however, the home is the centre of the life of the great majority of Englishwomen. The Englishwoman is "house-proud," that is to say, she likes her home to look nice and to be well-kept. In cases where this is only possible if she will lend a hand herself, she does not mind how hard she works—which is so much the more in her favour, since she has a great dislike of cooking and washing and mending. No Englishwoman ever regards this kind of work as anything but a necessary evil or dreams of taking a real pride in it. For this reason she will drop housework as soon as ever circumstances make it possible for her to do so. A whole-time servant will be maintained in cases where a German family of equal income would make do with an occasional "help." The higher her social level the less does the English-woman do in the house beyond giving orders. Like her male counterpart, she seems born rather to rule than to serve.

Like him, she is naturally of a practical disposition. If put to it the Englishwoman knows very well how to economize under these circumstances; she always starts by economizing on food and heating, making sure that there is enough money left over for education, clothing, and amusements. Shabby clothes are always a sign of poverty, whereas icy-cold, draughty rooms, and scanty meals are not. An English husband will put up with things that would lead to a family quarrel in Germany. Nevertheless, economy as an end in itself bores the Englishwoman. If her husband's income is too small, she sees no reason why she should not seek some means of adding to it by her own earnings. Wherever possible she prefers to engage help in the house in order to leave time for more interesting and lucrative occupa-tions. Almost anything seems to attract her more than housework.

It is not therefore surprising that as a housekeeper the Englishwoman lags behind her German sister. Given the same income and the same purchasing power of money, a German family lives better than the English one. In times of difficulty, however, the Englishwoman pulls herself together and appears at her best. As by a miracle she will suddenly throw off self-seeking and fight like a tigress for her family, whether it be by the labour of her own hands or by marshalling her social

THE ENGLISHWOMAN

and personal connections in the interests of her husband. Many a home has been saved from poverty by the fact that the wife has engineered some necessary business introduction. Her moral courage in such cases is unbounded. The Englishwoman thoroughly enjoys sharing her husband's struggles. Every year hundreds of Englishwomen follow their menfolk to the most inhospitable of foreign shores and share as a matter of course in dangers and privations. Meanwhile the children are left behind in England. The pages of English history are full of the deeds of male "empire-builders." But their exploits should not cause the heroism of their feminine partners to be forgotten.

The best English marriages are characterized by this capacity for companionship between husband and wife. It explains the great measure of freedom that each one leaves to the other, and the lack of jealousy that would be unthinkable in Latin countries. Indeed, the marriages in which men and women ask nothing but companionship of one another are the happiest in England. Complications set in only when mental, moral, or physical claims are made which the other partner is incapable of satisfying. It is only necessary to look into the faces of many Englishwomen in order to see the tragedy of unfulfilled longing beneath a mask of indifference; and the more feminine the woman is, the more clearly does this show itself. The "good companion" does not feel that she is missing anything. She is quite ready for her husband to spend his weekends on the golf-course and to prefer the society of his friends to that of herself. She simply grows a shade harder through this married bachelor existence.

It is otherwise with the type of woman who wishes to have and to keep the love of her husband when nature failed to endow him with the talents of a lover. Undoubtedly upbringing, temperament, and religion will in very many cases lead to resignation. But if not, the wife may seek to find outside marriage what marriage has denied her. She will hurl herself into the whirl of gaiety which the wealthy Londoner enjoys, dance until far into the night, and drink more cocktails than are good for her. The seventh commandment will have no more terrors for her. As in many other cases, equality of rights for women in England has been extended to cover sexual morality, at all events in the upper classes, though the middle class has remained more or less true to the ideals of its Victorian forbears.

The unmarried girl is as free in her own way as the married woman. At sixteen or seventeen her education is finished and she then has the right to have "a good time." This is true for all classes of society, even in cases when the girl is obliged to earn her own living. It is regarded as a matter of course that every girl should have her "boy friend" and should be more or less permanently in love. No secret is made of it and people talk quite openly about these love-affairs. It does not harm a girl's reputation in the least. She would be much more likely to be criticized by her parents if she failed to cherish any warmer feelings for one of her admirers. Flirtation is a recognized institution in English life. "We are going out for the day—bring your young man along," is a perfectly right and proper form of invitation. Moreover, a girl may spend the whole evening dancing with the youth of her choice without its giving rise to any gossip. The older generation agrees that a young woman should start early to sharpen her weapons for the great struggle with man. She must learn to stand on her own feet, to distinguish the true from the false, to be able to say yes and no tactfully. Thus flirtation becomes a great school of life in which the two sexes get to know one another, in order that they may one day be capable of choosing the right partner for themselves. The Englishman disapproves profoundly of made marriages. Hence girls are given the opportunity of gaining experience. There is no question but that this privilege was abused during the early post-war years. At that time seventeen-year-old girls went alone to dances and nightclubs, and arrived home in a state of intoxication. But since then a reaction has set in, and some sort of chaperonage has become customary again for girls in their first and second seasons.

Despite freedom and amusements, however, the life of the English girl is not free from care for the future. If the wealth of the country and the standard of living be taken into account, the Englishwoman is badly off. The reason is that it is much less usual to divide family property among all the children than is the case on the Continent. French or German parents will often make considerable sacrifices in order to give their daughters a good dowry. Not so the English, who are of opinion that each generation should look after itself and the husband provide for the wife. Finally, among the aristocracy as a result of the law of primogeniture the eldest son takes the lion's share of an estate, leaving only the meagrest crumbs for his sisters. Thus the daughters even of wealthy parents may be provided with nothing more than pocket-money by their parents when they marry. But even this amount, let alone a "marriage settlement," will be found to be customary only in a very small section of the population. It may therefore be said that the choice of practically every English girl lies between some calling and marriage. True, marriage is made easier for her in that the Englishman has a rooted objection to marrying for money, so that girls who are rolling in wealth may remain unmarried while the poorest may contract a brilliant alliance. In so far as material questions are concerned, the English woman is more calculating than the English man. Not heiresses but "eligible bachelors" are the golden calves worshipped in the market-place. A house in the country, a house in London, the social position, and possibly the title that the rich young man has to offer are too tempting.

Few have such a rosy future to look forward to. The great majority of English girls expect to work; those of the labouring classes in factories, those of the middle classes in shops or offices, and even in well-off families the girls are often expected to earn at least their own pocket-money. Many a young beauty who spends her evenings as a shining light in Society has spent the day designing furniture or dresses or working in a hat-shop. On the other hand, it is not customary for girls in Society to become nurses, nor to act as companions. In other ways, however, women are no longer as in Victorian times forbidden to earn money. Women are admitted to the universities, and the ban on the theatre has long since been lifted. Women and girls of all classes throng to the stage and to filmstudios. It was permissible for Winston Churchill's daughter, who would be a princess if she lived in Germany, to dance in a revue without compromising her social position or her prospects of marriage. If even a Churchill cannot refuse his consent, how much less possible is it for the average parent whose daughter suddenly discovers histrionic talents? More often than not such talents consist in a pretty face and a slim figure. If nature has provided them, so much the better. If not, cosmetics and starvation diets will help—and not only in the case of a theatrical career. Women and girls in England know of no higher commandment than that which bids them look their best. It is fortunate for them (and for Elizabeth Arden) that the English ideal of beauty has changed. In the old days ethereal loveliness or a classical profile were sought after. Nowadays it is better to be "attractive" or to have "sex appeal." A mouth that would have been looked upon as much too large fifty years ago will be made even larger by the use of lipstick. A figure that grandmamma would have criticized as not full enough will be "fined down" by strict dieting even if health suffers in the process. The dressmaker's art also prefers to emphasize the boyish, individual, and whimsical note to-day. Long past is the time when Englishwomen drifted through the world in sack-like garments, bedizened with glass beads and wearing shoes many sizes too large. The young generation dresses very well indeed, and if it does not achieve the *chic* of the Frenchwoman, at least the English country and sports clothes are superior to the French. Even the sense of colour—hitherto not the Englishwoman's strong point—has been awakened.

Manners have changed to harmonize with the change in appearance. The "dreamy beauty" type is dying out. In former times it was looked upon as poetic—nowadays as merely tiresome. Similarly, prudishness and stiffness no longer count as virtues. If Miss 1937 wishes to please, she must be a "good sport," must be gay and quick-witted, must not be afraid of horses, aeroplanes, or racing cars, must be ready to join in whatever is proposed. She must never be a spoil-sport, whatever situation may arise. The ideal is not the *jeune fille* with one eye always on her mother, but the girl who looks at life with both eyes, and who for all she is enterprising has an instinct for what is right. It is this which distinguishes the young Englishwoman from the Americanized version whose triumphal march in the early post-war years was of short duration.

By the early twenties, that is to say, comparatively young, the greater number of English girls are married. Then comes a time of tragi-comic experiment in housekeeping. Training for it is practically non-existent in a country in which it is not the custom to send girls to schools of cookery or domestic economy. The Englishwoman has to learn by practice how to run a house; and it must be said to her credit that as a result of her natural adaptability she does learn it comparatively quickly. Moreover, the gallant English husband is always ready to lend a hand, and science continues to provide an ever-increasing variety of labour-saving appliances and tinned foods. Nevertheless, England is looking with some concern at the domestic dilettanti who are becoming a real problem in the working classes. The greater the number of girls who go straight from school to factories, the greater the number of those who are incapable of making a home for their husbands. Hence the German example of domestic training is beginning to be followed in England at least among the poorer classes.

When an English girl marries she plans to have two or three children. Any greater number of offspring is prevented by "birth control," especially among the well-to-do. The reasons alleged vary from the frivolous one that "it is bad for the figure" to the well-intentioned, but—as has been shown by English statisticians—politically dangerous one that "we could not possibly give a decent education to any more." The ideal is that every English child shall be sent out into the world so prepared that he has good prospects of making his way. No one is to be dependent upon anyone else. Notwithstanding the affection that exists between the members of English families, the family bond is much looser than in France. There are no grandmothers and aunts in England to lay down the law at family councils. Indeed, if ever there is a clash of opinion between two generations, as often as not the younger will come off best. In any case, a certain reserve is maintained between parents and children. Moreover, the various members of the family are influenced by their natural liking for each other. Just as a woman is her husband's comrade, so she is her children's and especially her grown-up sons', who are all the more ready to ask the advice of a clever, experienced mother since it is not forced upon them. Such a relationship between a mother and her grown-up sons is one of the finest aspects of English family life,

D

33

for its success depends upon courage and tact. Courage is required to be a mother in a world-empire, when sons often have to be brought up in boarding-schools far removed from their homes, and later are scattered over the face of the earth. The Englishwoman can never have visions of herself as a matron with her children all gathered about her. She knows that she must soon be prepared to say farewell to them, perhaps for years at a time. For this reason English families who are not united by any natural inclination towards each other may drift apart and lose sight of each other in a way unimaginable on the Continent. Moreover, anyone who is not a member of the immediate family is not really part of the family at all. Nephews or uncles as such have no special claim to consideration unless they happen to be loved as friends. Very much more seldom than on the Continent are poor relations supported, though friends who happen to fall on evil times are gladly given a helping hand. Only in Scotland, where the clans form mighty family associations, does the call of the blood that has grown so faint in England still make itself heard.

To a certain extent this means that the proverb which says that the Englishman's home is his castle has lost its force. English family life has become looser: in a good sense in so far as it has grown freer and fresh air has blown away old cobwebs; in a bad sense in so far as the family no longer offers support to members who need help. The bond of blood has become a bond of utility, to be tightened or loosened as seems best. The number of divorces is increasing, even if not to the same extent as in the United States. None the less, the number of those who are not fitted for marriage is growing. The man who neglects his wife for the sake of his business and sport has been mentioned. But the change in marriage ideals cannot be attributed to men alone. The wealthier classes in England are full of vain, superficial women who have no idea beyond rushing from one amusement to the next. Equally irritating is the type of woman who is determined to appear "intellectual" and who is upon familiar terms with every kind of "ism," to the extent that she has forgotten how to be natural. In contrast to the English man, who—apart from a few young fools from Oxford —acts naturally, the English woman is not free from the danger of affectation. She is guilty, too, of a certain love of sensation—again in contrast to the English man— to say nothing of a liking for display and extravagance.

Nevertheless, if the Englishwoman's faults are analysed it will be found that they are chiefly derived from one source—her great urge to action. She is always doing something, carrying out real or imagined duties, throwing herself into amusements, running meetings, or hobbies. This eternal rush sometimes leads to hysteria and sometimes to a spiritual void. Or when her activities are devoted to more serious ends, they may destroy her womanly charm and make her hard and masculine as so many old maids are in England. It may turn the mother into the "sporting woman," whose only idea of life is fox-hunting and bridge. On the other hand, England owes much to the energy of its women. For although the Englishman is not lazy, he is inclined to be easy-going. While this characteristic may prevent his ruining his nervous system by overwork, it is also responsible for the fact that it is difficult to make the Englishman accept new ideas. In these circumstances it is most fortunate that England should breed women who are ready to stir up the country's unduly peaceful mental backwaters. The Englishwoman did a tremendous amount during the War. It brought out her passionate patriotism. No one realized this more keenly than did Lord Northcliffe, whose propaganda was with real genius adapted also to women, without whose hysteria the intoxication of hate[1] to which England abandoned itself during the war years would hardly have been possible, and which surprised no one more than the soldier returning from the front. It is only fair to add, however, that the Englishwoman did not confine her war-work to anti-German propaganda. The most luxurious ladies donned the nurse's uniform and carried on their work at the risk of their lives. The same class of women took to driving heavy lorries during the general strike of 1926. Frenchwomen may be more feminine than English, and Germans more maternal, but if ever England is threatened by dangers from within or without its women will be a reservoir of strength upon which the Empire may draw. Whoever the foe may be, the Englishwoman will be a terrible enemy, comparable with any man for courage, self-sacrifice, and tenacity. The difference in the nature of the

[1] [PUBLISHERS' NOTE.—Some of us who knew England during the War saw very little sign of this "intoxication of hate," which seems to have been engineered into a tradition during the last few years. Perhaps, too, the Germans did not spend so much of their time in singing Lissauer's notorious "Hymn of Hate" and in gloating over obscene cartoons directed against the English as some newspapers of the period would have had us believe.]

sexes is less clearly defined here than in other countries. The English man is not free from feminine traits, and in artistic and intellectual circles, especially, effeminate men are not infrequently to be met with. The English woman, for her part, will have to be careful lest energy and a desire for action should lead to her becoming masculine. This type of womanhood is in curious contrast to the astonishingly beautiful women who are still to be found in great numbers more especially in the ranks of the aristocracy. Despite a modern tendency to bring everything down to a dead level, Gainsborough and Reynolds would still find plenty of models in England to-day worthy of their art and worthy of the ancient fame that is justified in every generation of the beauty of the women of England.

CHAPTER III

CHILDHOOD, SCHOOL, AND COLLEGE

THE English agree with the Jesuits that education cannot begin too early. Who wants to be an Englishman has to start early. Even in its cradle a child is treated as might be expected in this country. It is given plenty of fresh air and water and is by no means over-indulged. No expense is spared, even in families where pence count. If at all possible, a nurse is engaged—the "Nanny" who plays such an important part in English families. Her sway in the nursery is absolute. Her authority may be greater even than that of the mother, for she has, when all is said and done, more experience. Though as a rule the Englishman does not care for specialists, he prefers an expert in the nursery. The advantages of the system may be proved by watching the succession of clean, rosy, delicious babies being wheeled through any of the parks. It is necessary to go into the slums to find a dirty or badly kept child.

The same care is expended on the choice of children's clothes as on those of their parents. Convention ordains precisely what a young man shall wear from the moment he stands on his own feet. Special shops cater for children's clothes, which must be attractive and practicable while never pandering to a love of display. The kind of dressed-up child that may be met with in the streets of France and Italy is unknown in England. In this country a child is allowed freedom of movement, which implies well-fitting, warm, well-ventilated clothing. At the same time the English child is expected to learn self-respect and self-confidence, and these virtues are not engendered by letting him run about ragged and disreputable. The English are the best and most sensibly dressed people in the world, and they begin to cultivate the art in their nurseries.

Even when parents have not much time to spend with their children, they bring them up excellently. This is largely due to the well-balanced nature of the English temperament, which prevents them from spoiling their children at one moment and bullying them the next. The natural authoritativeness of the Englishman shows the child exactly how far it can go. And, above all, the Englishman, who never quite loses his capacity for play, has a great gift of sympathy with the young mind. This enables him to find easy access to his child, and thus to the means of guiding and forming its character. The more tactfully this is done, the more effective it is; and the fewer punishments that are meted out the better. On no account must the development of the child's self-confidence be obstructed, nor obedience degenerate into servility. No Englishman expects his children to render instant obedience. If he finds any obduracy, he will exhaust his persuasive methods before having recourse to command. Once an order has been given, however, there is no going back on it. The child must learn that life is not always easy, and that it is wiser to control oneself than to run one's head against a stone wall.

As a rule, the Englishman likes to see his child display courage and independence, and is ready to overlook an impertinent answer if it shows character. The idea of fear, especially physical fear, must never be allowed to enter a child's mind. Hence boys and girls of five will be sent galloping across the fields on horseback at the risk of even serious falls. And many a continental mother would be horrified at the icy rooms in which the children even of rich people sleep. While every care is taken of them, children are brought up on Spartan principles in order that they may become hardy in mind and body. For this reason children are wherever possible sent to play out-of-doors in preference to indoors. It is better for a child to have sturdy arms and legs than to be able to recite poetry to his assembled family.

The child thus learns partly in earnest and partly in play what he will need through life. But the Englishman would not be true to type if manners and forms did not take first place in his scale of values. "Manners maketh man" is England's most famous educational slogan. But manners and customs are good only if they are natural and have become part of a person's individuality. Hence it is never too early to begin teaching the English child the conventions of English life, until they have become so much a matter of course that he is incapable of acting apart from them. An English father, who will not turn a hair if his son breaks a valuable piece of china, will be furious if the boy fails to open the door for his mother, or is rude to the postman, or does not help his baby sister in her first attempts at walking.

The efficacy of these educational methods is astonishing. Before young John has reached the stage of reading and writing he has acquired greater poise than continental children of three times his age. At the same time he is more modest. It is not good manners to push oneself forward. This is all part of the rule against attempting things beyond one's powers or supposing that one is marked out for a great destiny. Parents are careful not to hasten the course of their children's development beyond what is natural at any age. The result is a little person who is child-like and at the same time mature in his own way. The Englishman is an Englishman before he goes to his first school. He carries this precious and indestructible possession with him as he leaves the nursery.

A new and important stage in education, in the form of intercourse with others of his own age, is entered upon by an English child on his or her arrival at school. The Englishman is an avowedly social being and never overlooks the needs of society for all his individualism. Hence a child must learn as early as possible to fit into its niche and to make its own way. In the upper classes, especially, this is regarded as being of such importance that children are sent away from home at a very youthful age in order that they may learn at school to fit themselves for the state and society of adult life. England is a land of boarding-schools, although their high cost makes them accessible to a relatively small section of the population. Between the ages of five and fourteen the great mass of the people go to elementary schools where education is free. Books and other materials are also provided free of charge. While the educational scheme is to all intents and purposes similar to that followed in Germany, the social standard is different. Anyone who can possibly afford to do so sends his children not to an elementary school but to one of the private schools in which a large part of English education is carried on. Primitive as many of these private schools are, they are considered to be socially superior to the free schools. People with rather more money may have their children taught the first lessons at home, and will then send them to a preparatory school between the ages of eight and thirteen. The majority of these are also private schools, charging from thirty pounds to sixty pounds a year for tuition only and from one hundred and twenty pounds to two hundred pounds a year for boarders.

The preparatory school prepares boys for the public schools of which England is so proud that every successful enterprise is said to have been won in their classrooms and on their playing-fields. Nevertheless, it is a curiosity of nomenclature that these schools should be called "public." The most famous of them are anything but public. Despite scholarships, bursaries, etcetera, that are intended to lessen their plutocratic character, they are in the highest degree exclusive. There are not many fathers who can afford to pay the three hundred pounds or four hundred pounds that a year's schooling at Eton costs. Though the other great English schools, such as Harrow, Winchester, Rugby, Marlborough, and Stowe, are cheaper, they are beyond the means of the average man. He must be content to send his sons to one of the less known public schools or grammar schools. These establishments offer the same education, but lack the fame of the great schools and the corporate spirit that unites their pupils for the rest of their lives.

When the English schoolboy has spent five years at his preparatory school and three at a public school, he enters—usually at about the age of sixteen—for the examination for the School Certificate. Two more years and another examination is necessary for the Higher School Certificate, though this does not automatically open the doors of the universities to him. In many cases the universities can and do insist upon an entrance examination, a precaution that is rendered necessary by the differences that exist between various English schools and their teaching staffs whose members are not government officials, and whose qualifications are not necessarily subject to very severe tests. This is especially the case in the numerous private schools, where the teachers are frequently reminiscent of the school-slaves of ancient Greece. It is only by slow degrees and against immense opposition that the Board of Education is succeeding in bringing some sort of uniformity into the educational system. To this end "suggestions" are sent to the municipal or county councils who are in charge of the schools. Even the power of the Board of Education, however, fails before the special privileges enjoyed by many of the older schools which possess considerable private property and their own governing bodies who watch jealously over their rights. Whichever happens to be the highest school-authority, its chief task is to appoint the head-master. Once the appointment has been made, the headmaster becomes veritable lord over life and death within his domains, and may within very wide limits order them as he thinks best. Not merely may he treat his staff as he chooses, but the scheme of work and the school regulations, in short, everything that gives the school its character, are at his discretion. The lesser schools naturally tend to a relative measure of uniformity, but the greater and older schools insist upon their own individuality that finds purely external expression in the top hats of Eton and the straws of Harrow. The headmasters of these schools are more than merely local lights. They are national figures, and are called into consultation upon all important educational questions.

As the headmaster is among the staff, so is the head boy in the school. He is the actual link between master and boys, he must be both inspector and diplomat, and is responsible for keeping the other boys in some sort of order. Only if the head boy fails does the master deal with the situation. This important young man is chosen not on account of intellectual attainments, but on account of the confidence that he enjoys among boys and masters. Here we have an excellent example of that training in leadership which is looked upon as so important in England and for which the foundations are laid as early as possible. While other countries took for their motto "Knowledge is power," the English always realized the danger inherent in knowledge not backed by character. Hence they were most careful not to overload young minds without at the same time strengthening the youthful will. They preferred sturdy young barbarians to "swots" or "molly-coddles." In view of the fact that such ideals are held, it is not surprising to find that corporal punishment has survived in English schools. Even fifth-form boys may be given a thorough thrashing without thereby incurring disgrace so long as the culprit takes his punishment decently, that is to say, like a Red Indian at the stake.

Besides striving for harmony between brain and character English education also aims at achieving a wise balance between mind and body. In this sense, again, England was generations ahead of the rest of the world. No German classical master of pre-war days would have considered himself on a level with the physical training instructor. It was otherwise in England, where the classical man would very likely not have obtained his post but for some prowess on the sports ground. At his first interview the headmaster would have said to him: "That is where you can get into human touch with your pupils." The young Englishman is taught that his body has an inalienable right to be looked after. This idea is rubbed into him to such an extent that for the rest of his life he hardly ever fails to provide himself with the necessary amount of exercise. The English sportsman is also formed young, which explains the matter-of-course way in which games are played in England in comparison with countries which are newer to it. At school these are chiefly cricket and football, whereas the English have a strong aversion to gymnastics. So also walking—hiking—is a recent development. The barbarian element in the young Englishman does not enjoy the sentimental contemplation of Nature but the drama of competitive games. His teachers are satisfied that it should be so, for they realize that the boy will thereby learn the art of winning and losing gracefully, and that it is better to be a good loser than to be intoxicated by victory. Above all, games teach the sacrosanctity of the rules of the game. And everything in

England follows the rules of the game, from port wine which must pass clockwise round the table to parliamentary procedure. The English are economical with statutes graven upon stone. For everyday life the rules of the game, together with conventions as learnt at school, are enough.

Proud as the Englishman is of his schools, he is not blind to their shortcomings. Where such great stress is laid upon physical development, there is always the danger that a boy's mental alertness may begin to fail. The fact that so many grown-up Englishmen suffer not merely from mental indolence but also from an actual hostility to intellectual pursuits is to a great extent the fault of their school education. It is a serious matter when sixth-form boys will debate the function of music, and come to the conclusion that Bach and Beethoven come under the heading of amusements.

By its constant insistence on self-control and reserve school life also contributes to the suppression of spontaneity and to the growth of English coldness of manner. Nor are the snobbery and the plutocratic character of a system under which the school attended by a boy is an indication of the financial position of the father admirable. Germany, which has equally good and cheap schools in every town, is in this respect more democratic than England, where the schools are as different from one another as day and night, and where, at all events until a very few years ago, a good education was a luxury.

On the credit side of the balance, however, stands the fact that the English school has succeeded in creating a national type. Whatever may be thought of the type as such, its existence is one of England's great sources of strength. It is true that England is no more able than any other country to raise great men by wishing for them, but its average is always high. If, as has been said, England's success is due to a never-failing stream of men of high average capacity, this is to be attributed to the schools. They carry on parental education in a homogeneous manner, just as they form the homogeneous preliminary to the universities.

The homogeneity of English education is still further increased by the fact that the same young people are found at the universities as those who went to school together. From Eton and Harrow boys move *en bloc* to Oxford and Cambridge, where they spend the whole of their student days. The wandering scholar going from one university to another is unknown in England. Anyone who begins his studies in Oxford stays there to finish them. During this long period spent in living together friendships are formed which last for a lifetime. In England, where friendship is still regarded as in the eighteenth century as one of life's greatest boons, this opportunity for making friends is regarded as one of the main advantages of the school and university system. Many men send their sons to Oxford, not so much on account of the learning to be acquired there as for the friends they will make and the final polish that they will acquire.

Oxford and Cambridge have a two-fold character. In one sense they are technical schools like the German universities, but in contrast to these they are also schools of general culture. The son of a business man who intends joining his father's firm, the young nobleman who expects to inherit great estates, the prospective army officer, the future parliamentary candidate, all go to Oxford and Cambridge, but not to study law, economics, or diplomacy. They read history, literature, philosophy, and the natural sciences, in short, anything in which they are interested and by means of which they hope to round off their education. In this sense Oxford and Cambridge complete the work of the public schools. In view of the fact that the universities count men like Rutherford, Keynes, and many of the best brains in the world among their teaching staff, it is unnecessary to labour the point that they are also useful for those who wish to study for a profession.

The two-fold character of Oxford and Cambridge is lacked by the numerous other universities in England, to which young people are sent, as in Germany, purely for the sake of their professional studies. While, however, there is practically no difference socially between the various German universities, Oxford and Cambridge form a class apart in the academic life of England, and their undergraduates would take it very ill if they were put on a level with those of Leeds, Manchester, or Bristol. Oxford and Cambridge are the universities of the upper ten, for men whose fathers can afford to spend at least three hundred pounds a year on them. A certain leaven is introduced by means of bursaries and free scholarships, which are, it is true, very numerous.

Anyone who is fortunate enough to be sent to Oxford or Cambridge has, as the phrase goes, the happiest time of his life there. It may be the happiest, but it certainly is not the freest. Oxford and Cambridge are boarding-schools the inmates of which are obliged to be indoors by midnight and to have their studies supervised by what is called a tutor. The universities are a federation of colleges, each of which is a little university in itself, with its own teaching staff, its own administrative body, and its own finances. A youth does not become simply an Oxford undergraduate, but a Christ Church, Balliol, Trinity, Magdalen, or Jesus "man." The sacred names borne by so many of the colleges are a reminder of their monastic origins. To be admitted to these colleges is not a matter of course, nor altogether of passing an examination. Despite the admission of some non-collegiate students, space is limited. Hence anyone who wants to send his son to Oxford or Cambridge must put down his name in good time, which, incidentally, is true of the great public schools also. The future Etonian is entered as soon as he is born. Otherwise there is always the risk that by the time he is fourteen there may be no vacancy. Thus the limitation of number acts to some degree for all great educational establishments in England.

The young man who goes to Oxford or Cambridge must divide his days into three sections. The first, but by no means the most important, is devoted to study, the second to sport, and the third to society. While practically all forms of sport are indulged in, the one that numbers most adherents is rowing, with the annual race from Putney to Mortlake as its culminating point. Next in importance come cricket and football. The distinction which may be won by the best oarsmen, cricketers, or football-players is the "blue," so-called because of the blue cap that is worn by this company of the elect. An Oxford or Cambridge "blue" is the most

E 49

useful distinction that can be conferred on any sportsman in any part of the world. It acts as an "open
sesame" to all doors and is perhaps the best introduction
that a young man can start out with on his career. He
may end up as Prime Minister, Field-Marshal, or millionaire, but his obituary notice will never fail to
mention his "blue." To be a "blue" is something that
stamps a man for life; like the priestly consecration, it
can never be taken from him. Parents who are barely
interested if their offspring becomes a B.A. can hardly
contain themselves with pride if he achieves his "blue."
Generally they are quite right in thinking that they
need have no further concern for the young man's
future.

Nevertheless, it would be a mistake to consider
Oxford or Cambridge merely as a vast sports club.
Sport, too, is made to serve a higher end, to form a man
who can hold his own among his fellows. It is therefore
expected of every student that he shall make his contribution to the general life of the university. He is not
only obliged to attend communal meals, but must also
spend much time in the society of his friends. An
Oxford college thus resembles a beehive, the inmates of
which form one large family. Men spend hours upon a
neighbour's sofa, or go to breakfast with him—a
form of hospitality that is a speciality of the universities.
Beer and whisky, of course, also have their part in
English university life, though not in the form of
organized drinking parties. England has nothing to
compare with the German Students' Corps of the old
days. Their place is taken by clubs that are either
inherited ready-made from earlier generations or

founded anew as the necessity arises. Oxford and
Cambridge are full of clubs and societies, formed for
every conceivable purpose, from Russian and Chinese
literature, politics, and music to, more recently, the
study of social questions. Meetings of the associations
are the active complement of the passive work in the
lecture rooms. They teach the young man to formulate
and defend his knowledge and opinions. For this reason
debates are much indulged in, with proposers, opposers,
and divisions, exactly as in the House of Commons.
And so wide is the reputation of the great student
associations that grey-haired London statesmen do not
consider it to be beneath their dignity to take part in the
debates of nineteen-year-olds. Small wonder; for here
are the men who will later on fill the House of
Commons and become their own successors. They
cannot begin training them too soon. Many of England's politically gifted men have first made their mark
in the debating clubs of the universities, where the
special methods of English debating are regarded as an
art. Though by no means to the same extent as formerly,
there is even now a well-trodden path to Whitehall via
Oxford or Cambridge. England's ruling classes forge
the tools with which they have created the mightiest
democracy in the world in that small state within a
state. Thus it is understandable that half England was,
as it were, stunned when the Oxford Union carried the
motion that they would refuse to fight for king and
country. The publicity given to this resolution was a
typical instance of the English capacity for scenting
danger from afar. Let Communists and Socialists
demonstrate in Hyde Park in their thousands; that is all

part of the day's work. But if Oxford falters, then the foundations of English social order rock.

The eyes of a world-empire are fixed upon the young people who are training to fulfil their political tasks at Oxford and Cambridge, despite the growing competition of non-academic men. A cheerful and carefree spirit, nevertheless, reigns in the places where England brings up its sons. Another example of the Spartan régime may be mentioned here. No Oxford or Cambridge undergraduate ever wears hat or overcoat. Grey flannel trousers and a disreputable sweater are the average man's dress, while a black gown is prescribed for lectures and meals in hall. Anyone who insists upon presenting a dandified appearance does so at the risk of being ducked. The only peculiarity allowed is the Oxford accent, a drawling, somewhat blasé manner of speech. Apart from this, the richest and highest-born young men are at pains not to appear too rich or too highly-born during their college days.

Oxford and Cambridge bring the young Englishman's education to an end. If he is not an Englishman by this time, he will never be one. But in cases where Oxford and Cambridge have fulfilled their mission—and they are probably the greatest educational forces in the world, together with the Jesuit monasteries and the Prussian Officers' Corps—the Englishman has received an indelible impress. No Englishman ever forgets this period in his life. It is only necessary to hear an old Oxford or Cambridge man speak of his undergraduate days to realize from the tone of his voice what these places have meant to him. Over and over again it has been the profoundest experience of his whole life.

Oxford and Cambridge could not work these miracles were they not themselves a hundred per cent. English, the inimitable repositories of centuries of tradition and culture. This is expressed even in the architecture of the two cities. Gothic and Renaissance have united to make Oxford and Cambridge into pearls of European architecture, with the green lawns of England and the splendid old trees as Nature's contribution. And inside the colleges panelled halls and wonderful old pictures and furniture teach the young Englishman to be proud of the traditions of his country.

Within this unique framework, which the numerous ecclesiastical structures of Oxford and Cambridge render still more picturesque, England's privileged youth spends the most impressionable years of its life. The English must be barbarians—which they are not—did not these, in the best sense of the words, poetic surroundings stir the profounder deeps of their souls. However much time may be devoted to sport and politics, the universities, and especially Oxford, have over and over again been the nursery of fresh artistic, religious, or ethical movements. Their undergraduate periodicals, in which the young men publish their poems, essays, and criticisms, need fear no comparison with any student-organ in the world. Nor must it be forgotten how much the two universities have done for the advancement of learning, wherein the fame of Oxford rests mainly upon classical and historical research and that of Cambridge upon scientific and mathematical.

It is an obvious result of the college system that women could not become members of the great colleges when they were admitted to academic studies. Special colleges were therefore founded for them, such as Lady Margaret Hall and St. Hilda's at Oxford. The "undergraduette"—who looks extremely well in cap and gown—spends her student days in these colleges in much the same way as her male counterpart, from whom she is kept strictly separate.

Even England could only produce two such universities as Oxford and Cambridge, in comparison with which the numerous other universities are colourless. They lack the power to stamp their pupils with a specific character. Like similar continental institutions, they are places where people go to learn and they hardly trouble about the creation of a particular social type. At the same time London, Edinburgh, St. Andrew's, or Bristol, to take only the best known, are excellent universities and in many ways more progressive than the "Mecca and Medina." It is, moreover, inevitable that with the desire for education of new sections of the people who cannot afford Oxford or Cambridge the importance of these other universities should increase. The number of their students is rising annually, and they are able to point with pride to their industry and successes in examinations. Much fresh blood is thus brought into England's intellectual life. But this means at the same time that an "intellectual proletariat" comes into being, which misfortune England has hitherto been spared owing to the high cost of education. Since this cost is now being reduced, England is faced with the problem of finding a middle way between the ideal of a good education for everyone and the danger of overproduction of university men. For even in England unemployed and dissatisfied university men tend to revolutionary parties. If these find foothold in Oxford, how much more so in places where even the university years are famine years? In so far as it has widened its educated class, England has created problems that were unknown to the fathers and grandfathers of the present generation. There is no going back. Only progress wisely planned and directed can lead to a solution.

CHAPTER IV

THE SOCIAL STRUCTURE

OF all the European Great Powers England is the one whose social system has been least affected by the War. There have been neither inflation nor a fascist or communist revolution to disorganize it. Despite changes, which England has escaped no more than other places, the social order has remained fundamentally as it was. England is a land of classes, though not in quite the same sense as imperial Germany or Austria, where there were four classes—nobility, bourgeoisie, peasantry, and workmen. The situation in England is different, where it has proved possible to unite a class system with democracy.

To take first the English working class, it is interesting to note that it refuses to be called a "proletariat." "Proletarian" remains an alien word, with no significance for the Englishman. Nor do the English working classes regard themselves as a distinct section of the population, or consider that they have been defrauded of life. They certainly realize that their conditions of life are unfavourable and form associations for their amelioration or for introducing social reforms. But this does not imply that they look upon members of other classes as permanent antagonists. While the General Strike was in progress the strikers played football with the police, and the footballs were provided by the capitalist owners of factories. And at the time of King George V's Jubilee, the very poorest parts of London made the most touching efforts to achieve really festive decorations. The King conveyed his recognition by the royal gesture of paying these particular districts a special, unexpected visit.

Only the future will show whether political agitators will some day succeed in destroying the powerful unity of this people. At present there is no atmosphere of class-warfare. This is clear to anyone who comes in contact with English working people and the poorer classes generally. The courtesy that is met with among these classes is unsurpassable, and is in the sharpest possible contrast to the unfriendly tone in which, for example, a Parisian proletarian will reply to anyone who is better dressed than himself. London's poorer classes are re-nowned for their humour, the famous Cockney humour.

The politeness of the English working classes does not mean that they are resigned to their fate. Since the end of the last century the masses of the workers have begun to move, and despite considerable set-backs they are advancing. Under this pressure social welfare has made great progress, though it has not yet achieved the German level. Only the housing movement, having for its object the providing of each family with its own home, is more advanced in England than in Germany, owing to the greater amount of money at the disposal of the English authorities, and thus the boundaries between the working classes and the lower middle classes become increasingly indeterminate. On the other hand, there is no "Kraft durch Freude" (Strength through

Joy) organization in England, and the German workman is better protected than his English prototype against the fluctuations of the markets. As regards factory hygiene and safety regulations, again the comparison results in Germany's favour. And long before the House of Commons was debating the question of paid holidays for work-people, they had been introduced in Germany. It is true that the highly skilled workman, who earns between four pounds and five pounds a week in England, is probably better off than the equally skilled German. But he forms only a minute fraction of the working class, which in England especially consists of a very large proportion of unskilled labour, both male and female. Hence within the working classes, as within the whole nation, the variations in income are probably sharper than in Germany. England has only partially learnt the art of improving the lot of the less fortunately situated by means of organization. It must be added, however, that England is engaged upon a programme of social reform which is being carried out with increasing rapidity every year.

While a comparison is possible between the English and German urban working classes, it is quite impossible between the peasantry of the two countries. The English agricultural workers have sunk so low that it is hardly possible nowadays to describe them as a social class. This point will be discussed in a later chapter. There is, therefore, no need to elaborate it here.

Hence there remain the nobility and the middle classes, two of the most involved structures known to European sociology. It used to be quite easy to tell who belonged to which of these two classes in Germany.

Not so in England, which has nothing corresponding either to the German *Bürger* or the French *bourgeois*, and which generally describes its nobility—or what it understands by this term—not as nobility or aristocracy, but as upper classes. At the same time the words upper classes do not refer solely to the aristocracy. There is a very clear line of demarcation between the upper classes and the middle classes, though the distinction is hard to formulate. The foreigner usually makes the mistake of thinking that the difference lies in the title, whereas titles really mean very little. Innumerable middle-class people go through life as Sir and Lady, while highly-born aristocrats are merely plain Mr. and Mrs. An Englishman may even wear a peer's coronet and his wife may attend royal functions in a diamond tiara without their being reckoned among the aristocracy on that account. Finally, Esq., the contraction of Esquire, is simply a courtesy title, used only on letters and legal documents.

All this seems very complicated to the foreigner and may lead to the oddest social mistakes, but it is settled instinctively by the Englishman. His instinct tells him what anyone else's social position is, without any inquiry as to the stranger's name or style. For the upper and middle classes are not two classes so much as two different attitudes to life, which are expressed in manner, taste, form of speech, and the French *je ne sais quoi*. "I can't give you the definition of an elephant," a witty Englishman once said, "but I know one when I see it." What is true for the elephant is true for the distinction between the upper and middle classes, as also for that between what is a gentleman and what is not—which is not the same question. An earl may behave in such a manner that no one will call him a gentleman, while the son of humble parents may be numbered among gentlemen. There are plenty of other difficulties that may arise. A man is most likely to judge correctly who relies upon personal impressions. These will be of more use to him than all the Gothas in the world.

The lack of uniformity in the social and historical significance of English names and titles is due to the peculiar character of the House of Lords, which is at once a hereditary, aristocratic Chamber and a continually renewed Senate. At New Year, on the King's birthday, at any change of Government, tradition prescribes that titles shall be showered upon the English people. Many of these are purely tactical elevations in rank, as, for instance, if the Cabinet wishes to elevate a particular Minister to the Upper House or to silence an awkward critic. A truly grotesque situation arose when the Labour Party came to power and it was necessary for it to be represented in the House of Lords. It was then that the Labour Peer, before his elevation usually the sworn foe of the Upper House, came into existence. A few years earlier Lloyd George had created the Newspaper Peer, who has now been followed by the Automobile Peer. This was no more than a logical development of the old practice of translating the great industrial leaders of the country to the Upper House. All ranks of the English peerage contain a considerable proportion of merchant princes. Very little remained of the old feudal nobility after the members of it had practically anni-hilated one another in the Wars of the Roses, and since then the action of the law of primogeniture has hastened the extinction of families. Hence families like the Derbys, Nevilles, and Norfolks may be counted on one's fingers. And even in cases where—as with the Warwicks—there appears to be a historical background, further investigation will reveal either that there is no connection with the ancient bearers of the name or that the connection is only through the female line. Once a title dies out the name is free, and a new peer may adopt it upon his creation. Thus there is no distinction between the ancient and the more modern nobility in England, where a family tree going back one hundred and fifty to two hundred years is considered to be old.

Money and ambition pave the way to the House of Lords just as much to-day as in earlier times. Nearly anyone who has amassed sufficient wealth can force the doors of the Upper House, whether by means of charitable foundations or by friendship with the Party in power. Some such reason as "Public Services" will be found to preserve the outward semblance of good form. This is not necessary where public services have actually been rendered; these are rewarded by the conferment of titles in England as in other monarchical countries. If a Cabinet Minister or an Ambassador is anxious to become a peer there will be no difficulty about it when he retires, to say nothing of Generals and Admirals after a victorious war. Even an isolated service may be rewarded in this manner, as, for instance, when a great industrial magnate or banker volunteers to act as chairman to a Royal Commission. In this manner the Government receives valuable assistance at no cost to itself.

The result of this system is that the English aristocracy is by no means restricted in its numbers. On the contrary, it is continually being renewed. Fresh blood is infused year by year, while it deposits in the ranks of the untitled its own younger sons and their sons. This interchange, which is beneficial to both parties, is further increased by the fact that when an English nobleman marries he hardly troubles to consider his wife's genealogy. Within certain very wide limits a peer may marry whom he will, and beauty is regarded as a veritable patent of nobility. Not a few of the bearers of the highest titles began life as chorus-girls. So long as the lady adapts herself to her new position, nobody will remember her antecedents. The English aristocracy is not snobbish nowadays; indeed, arrogance is looked upon as bad form, as also is the question frequently asked by foreigners as to the maiden name of Lady So-and-so. Once a girl is married, her maiden name is forgotten, being never used on visiting cards or other documents. People are Lord or Lady, just as they have blue eyes or brown ones. The less said about it the better.

And this aristocracy, an aristocracy that is sedulous to lay as little stress as possible upon its rank, is adored by the English people. For it is the people, not the nobility, that tends to snobbery. The mayoress of a small town will blush with joy at shaking hands with a countess, who does so as a matter of course, while her husband the earl does not think himself too grand to play cricket on Saturday afternoons with his own servants. The tact of the English nobility is the foundation of the enormous prestige it enjoys in its own country, which is glad to use it for that form of representation for which it is fitted by birth and upbringing. No bazaar, no exhibition, no charitable affair, no function of any description is possible without its aristocratic patrons. Even the City, sober and business-like as it is, adorns its boards of directors with the bearers of great names, recognizing that the public is powerfully impressed by them. In the same way the Press is not simply filling up space by publishing column after column describing the receptions and clothes, the travels and amusements of the aristocracy and Society. Fleet Street knows how much the suburbs enjoy mixing with the great on paper ; chiefly, of course, the women, to whose instincts of snobbery advertise. ments are also addressed. "The Countess of So-and-so (*who receives a handsome cheque for the revelation*) uses X Soap." The wives and daughters of thousands of little clerks will at once use the same soap.

The English are the first to make fun of their own snobbery, that provides their theatre with endless material for comedies. There was nothing to compare with it in old Germany, whose aristocracy preferred to be exclusive in a manner impossible to realize in England. Even clearer is the difference between the English aristocracy and the French, which has sat sulking in a corner ever since the fall of the monarchy, and let the State—which has no use for it either—go its own way. The English aristocracy takes a very active part in public life both in London and in the provinces. The pages of English history are full of the names of great noblemen, of the Derbys and the Devonshires, of Russells, Cecils, and Churchills, who have done invaluable service to their country. And this in spite of the immense wealth possessed by many of them. The English aristocracy is rich, which means in England having an income of at least five thousand pounds a year. And in a good many cases incomes are five times that amount. How long this will go on is, of course, a different question, when death duties may cost a man the half of his property and agriculture is growing progressively less profitable. If the aristocracy were dependent upon farming, it would, despite its enormous territorial possessions, that are far greater than those of the German aristocracy, have long since been bankrupt. The English nobility is saved from this by its participation in industry, by its ownership of urban house property, and by its work in the City. Many a great country house and park that is England's pride is preserved only because their owner is director of a company for five days a week. England has long ago abandoned the prejudice that a nobleman can only serve the king. The younger sons in particular have for generations sought and found their fortune in the City.

Despite socialist agitation the English people, the least envious in the world, do not grudge their aristocracy its wealth. They love the country houses and the parks, even if they are never—or only once a year for some charitable purpose—allowed to set foot in them. England is made more beautiful by its great estates, which are the expression of the grand manner of living. The ancient Prussian simplicity has never been recognized as an English ideal, and thus a peer who fails to live in accordance with his rank is reproached for his lack of good form. Aristocracy in England is a present-day fact and not a historical survival. Very few of the old privileges of peers have been preserved. Apart from their rank at Court, nothing much remains beyond the right to sit and vote in the House of Lords. The claim of a peer to be tried by his equals is too seldom made use of to count as an actual privilege. And even these privileges —including the peculiar right of being hanged with a silken rope in case of condemnation to death—only apply to the higher nobility. The lower ranks enjoy no privileges, hardly even that of calling themselves aristocratic. When they happen to be dowered with lands, they are called gentry, but they need bear no actual title in order to do so. In England even the division into greater and lesser nobility is to be taken with reservations. If for the sake of clearness the distinction is made here, it will be found that the lesser nobility consists almost only of baronets. The title of knight, with very few exceptions, such as Knight of Kerry and Knight of Glyn, is purely personal and not hereditary. This title is bestowed very freely upon successful doctors, actors, orchestral conductors, aldermen, judges, lawyers, the higher grades of naval and military officers. Men distinguished in this manner have the right to be called Sir; a title which, in so far as it is not merely a formal mode of address, is invariably attached to the Christian name. Thus Mr. Smith upon being dubbed knight does not become Sir Smith but Sir John Smith, and is always addressed socially as Sir John. The wife does not add the title to her Christian name. Sir John Smith's wife is Lady Smith, not, for example, Lady Margaret Smith. A baronet is similarly entitled, except that Bt. or Bart. is added to his name on letters and documents to distinguish him from the knight. A baronetcy is hereditary, but only by the eldest son. By creating this title, which goes back only to the year 1611, the Crown made it possible to distinguish men who wished to have a "handle" to their names without thereby losing the right to sit in the House of Commons. The doors of the Lower House are closed to a peer. Elevation to the House of Lords may therefore mean the end of a political career. Hence many men who are politically ambitious for themselves and their eldest sons content themselves with the low rank of baronet instead of aspiring to a peer's coronet.

Above the baronets comes the higher nobility, of which the heads of the families sit in the House of Lords, and which is divided into the following classes— Baron and Baroness, Viscount and Viscountess, Earl and Countess, Marquess and Marchioness, Duke and Duchess. Of these titles, that of Baron is only used on official documents, being replaced in every-day life by that of Lord. This is also the customary form of introducing other peers, with the exception of a Duke, who is introduced as the Duke of So-and-so. Finally, the modes of address "Your Lordship," "My Lord," and for a Duke "Your Grace" are never, except in official documents, used by social equals.

It is a fundamental law of the nomenclature of the upper nobility that only one person bears each title. The use of the title by all the members of the family, as in Germany, where Graf Dohna's five sons are all Graf Dohna, is an anomaly in English eyes. There is never more than one Lord Pembroke, whose Christian name is therefore never used. Moreover, a peer's title is usually not even his family name. The family name of

the Pembrokes, for instance, is Herbert, of the Rose-
berrys Primrose, of the Derbys Stanley. If Mr. Brown
is transferred to the Upper House, he does not usually
call himself Lord Brown, but takes the name of a place
with which he has some connection. Thus the great
lawyer and politician F. E. Smith became Earl of
Birkenhead. If a family goes up several stages in rank,
a change of name may occur every time. The older
titles in such cases are used for the eldest sons.

While only the peer and his wife use the title of the
peerage, their children have a prefix even during the
lifetime of the parents. In the case of a plain Lord, that
is to say, a Baron, The Honourable, shortened to The
Hon., is put before the Christian names of all the sons
and daughters, who, moreover, use the family name,
not the name of the peerage. Any children of the well-
known motor magnate Lord Nuffield would therefore
be known as The Hon. So-and-so Morris. The same is
true for a Viscount and his descendants. From Earls
upwards there is a change. All the daughters use the
prefix Lady, which in this case is always attached to the
Christian name. This title persists even in case of
marriage with an untitled person, so that an Earl's
daughter who married a Mr. Brown would be called
Lady Jane Brown. The eldest son of an Earl is a Lord
or Viscount, his younger brothers The Honourable.
Higher up again, the eldest son of a Marquess is an
Earl or Viscount, the younger ones Lord, while the
eldest son of a Duke uses the title of Marquess and the
younger sons that of Lord. Any variations that may
occur do so for some special historical reason or older
conferment of titles. "The Right Honourable," on the

other hand, is not a title of nobility. It is borne by English Ministers in their capacity as members of the Privy Council, and is used instead of the title Excellency, which is the prerogative of overseas governors and foreign ambassadors.

As a result of the unique system of nomenclature among the higher English aristocracy almost every member of a family may be called something different. To take as an example the Carlisles, who belong to the Howard family: the father and mother are Earl and Countess of Carlisle, the eldest son is Viscount Morpeth, the younger sons are The Hon. So-and-so Howard, the daughters Lady So-and-so Howard. In the next generation, the sons of The Honourable So-and-so Howard become plain Mr. Howard unless one of them happens to be raised to the peerage on his own merits. This happened in the case of the Marquess of Salisbury's third son, who was Lord Robert Cecil until he moved into the Upper House as Viscount Cecil of Chelwood. He thereby founded a new peerage, as the representative of which he occupies a seat in the House of Lords. Before that he was simply a younger son and his eldest brother represented the family in the House of Lords. Only the bearer of the title is a member of the House of Lords, leaving his sons and brothers free to be elected to the House of Commons. If Lord So-and-so is a member of the House of Commons it means that he is either a younger son or an eldest son whose father is living.

These younger sons deserve a page to themselves in the book of fame of English history. Over and over again, disinherited by the law of primogeniture, they have set out into the world and have there made a name for themselves that far outshone the direct line—as, for example, the great Duke of Wellington, who was born third son to the Earl of Mornington, of the Wellesley family.

Finally, the Scottish clans are a class apart. They are composed of members of the most various social classes, who are nevertheless united by the strongest possible clan-feeling. At the head of the clan is a chief, who may be a Duke, like the Duke of Argyll, the head of Clan Campbell, or may have a historic title like The Mackintosh of Mackintosh and Cameron of Lochiel. Until quite recently the great Clan Maclean, thirty thousand strong, possessed the finest "specimen" of a chief in Sir Fitzroy Maclean, who lived to be over a hundred years old.

Sandwiched between the great upper and lower classes lies England's most powerful class, the middle class, that calls itself the backbone of England. It does the commercial work of a nation of shopkeepers and conducts its administration. Of this class are England's doctors, civil servants, judges, clergy, lawyers, teachers, industrialists, as well as a considerable proportion of its politicians, army officers (with the exception of the Guards), and naval men. Mr. Baldwin [1] and his wife are middle-class people, and so are the Chamberlains—but not the Churchills nor Mr. Eden. Out of every hundred tourists travelling in foreign parts, ninety-nine are middle class, as also is the social sphere in which the average foreigner finds himself in England. Hence the

[1] The German edition of this book was published shortly before the announcement of Mr. Baldwin's peerage.

English people are judged far more by this class than by their nobility or peasantry. For good and ill. It is in the main the responsibility of the middle class if the Englishman is decried as stiff and cold, prudish, hypo-critical, and self-righteous. The faults of the upper class are less these than a lust for pleasure, frivolity, and a love of Mammon. The lack of taste displayed in English suburban houses, with their shoddy furniture, mauve carpets, ornaments, and lace covers, must be numbered among the sins of the middle classes, while England's upper class nowadays has perhaps the best taste in the world. Taste may be taken as the touchstone of the difference between the two classes. This is significant in a country in which classes in society are divided far more according to their mode of living than their genealogy. While the faults of the middle class are under discussion, mention must be made of one danger to which it is exposed—the tendency to be genteel, which is expressed especially in forms of speech. The dislike of the English for "refined" words and expressions goes so deep that there is a whole dictionary of "genteel-isms" to serve as a warning to all who wish to move in good society, whose nerves nothing irritates so badly as "gentility." Speech is the most dangerous rock to be negotiated by the social climber. Any echo of Suburbia or of Cockney speech and the newly-rich man is doomed, however luxurious his surroundings.

This is not to imply that the whole of the middle class is "genteel," has bad taste, and is distinguished for cold-ness. Nothing could be farther from the truth. Moreover, the middle class is graded into upper and lower middle class, with Galsworthy as the literary mouthpiece of the former. Though considerably laxer than in the days of Queen Victoria, the Forsytes are still the type of the upper middle class, which more or less corresponds to the higher *Bürgertum* in Germany. It is true that culture is a much more decisive indication of class in Germany than in England. No one thinks any the worse of a person in England because he knows nothing and has no intellectual interests. The intellectual side of life plays a smaller part, for the middle class is too much occupied with money-making and keeping up appearances. On the other hand, the English aristocracy, with its learned and artistic hobbies and its passion for collecting, is probably superior to the German in mental culture.

Numerous as may be the defects of the middle class, its good qualities are much more numerous. It is the strong framework that holds together not only a world-empire but also England's social structure by forming a broad band of transition from the very poor to the very rich. It may be less enterprising on the whole than its German counterpart, but makes up for it by quiet, imperturbable steadiness. Its pace determines that of the whole country, which likes work but not slavery, and which, despite its caution, is ready to risk a gamble on occasion—as witness the love of betting that runs through the whole nation from top to bottom. The Englishman is not like the Frenchman, who retires from business early, preferring to save more instead of earning more. The Englishman always likes to go on making money and improving his position. Hence the elderly English business man does not retire altogether but takes longer week-ends in the country and longer holidays: otherwise he keeps the reins in his own hands, even though his son and grandson may already be in the firm. Such good old family businesses bring a steadiness into English business life of which England has every reason to be proud; though it is true that they also introduce an element of stodginess.

It is obvious how much the honesty and fair dealing of the merchant classes must mean to a commercial nation like England. The administration is clean and self-respecting too; corruptions and scandals such as occur in France are unknown. Altogether, the civic virtues are to be found in abundance in the English middle classes, who do not work simply to fill their own pockets, but are also ready to put their whole hearts into working for the good of the parish, the county, the state, the Church, and the Empire. The English middle classes are patriotic to the point of Chauvinism. Foreign countries mean nothing to them. Foreigners are considered to be persons with doubtful principles. Especially in regard to sexual morality does the English middle-class person believe his country to be greatly superior to foreign lands. He still looks upon Paris as the world's worst sink of iniquity. This self-righteousness is not wholly without justification, for, taken all in all, English middle class family life must be admitted to be very happy. Nevertheless, there is no need to look as far as Paris to find laxity of conjugal morality.

England has always believed itself to be fortunate in possessing so broad a middle class. The decorative element in the country is perhaps to be sought elsewhere; that which is closest to the soil in again another part. But the base that gives the country its solidity and steadiness and enables it to develop with the minimum of upheavals is the middle class. It is the prop of government and commerce, of family and Church. Fundamentally it is Conservative, for it has no reason to complain of its fate. There is no higher class to oppress it, and it has sufficient opportunity for money-making to provide itself with an income commensurate with its needs. The way is also open for worldly advancement. The classes are not separated by any unscalable wall. Fresh arrivals are readily welcomed if only they will adapt themselves to the mode of life of their new friends. Hence England prefers never to mention its class distinctions, despite the fact that the differences in wealth are far more acute than they ever were in Germany. The middle class is very proud of its Lords and Ladies, whereas these ignore the class-distinctions by which they profit. Perhaps, indeed, this chapter is hardly to be considered as good form, because there has been so much discussion of class in it.

CHAPTER V

TOWN AND COUNTRY

THE population of England, Scotland, and Wales numbers forty-five millions, of which eight millions live in London. The remainder are divided among other large cities, numerous small towns, and the country districts. The chief distinction between Germany and England lies in the difference in the characteristics of the provincial towns. With few exceptions, such as Brighton, Eastbourne, Bath, and possibly Edinburgh, nobody lives in a provincial town unless their work obliges them to do so. There is nothing in England to compare with Weimar, Brunswick, or Freiburg, to which civil servants, army officers, and people with private incomes retire. Its provincial towns are either industrial places that everyone leaves as soon as he can afford to do so, or else market towns whose income is derived from the surrounding villages. London is the only real centre of cultural and social life. This is true despite the fact that the great industrial cities have of recent years become ambitious of possessing good theatres, art galleries, and orchestras, in the same way as places like Dortmund or Bochum. But no English provincial town has yet attained to the level of Düsseldorf, for example.

Hence people who want to be "in the swim" live in

London. If they do not care for London life, they have nothing to compare with Munich or Dresden or Stuttgart, where life is pleasant and cheap and there are excellent educational facilities for children. Hence they decide for the real country districts. But living in the country means something quite different in England from what it does in Germany, where such a mode of existence necessarily implies farming. Needless to say, there are plenty of agricultural estates in England too. But there is also an enormous number of country properties consisting of nothing except house and garden, far distant not only from any town but even from the nearest village. England is full of such freehold properties, the owners of which—provided they are not "gentlemen of independent means"—travel into town every day or several times a week for their work. In the neighbourhood of London such properties must, of course, approach one another more closely, even when they have not become actual colonies. But this is only because lack of ground space makes it inevitable. The better-off Englishman, except when he lives in London, never wishes to see any other houses. Otherwise he does not feel that he is really living in the country.

Townspeople own country estates of all sizes, from the modest bungalow or week-end cottage by way of the roomy country house to the great mansion standing in its own park. There may be large farms attached, or small ones, or none at all, or simply poultry and bees. Old farm-houses are especially favoured, and when they are fitted up with bathrooms and electric light they make the most picturesque and delightful dwellings. Since England has been preserved from invasion, a great number of old farm-houses have survived from previous centuries, with splendid dark oak beams and great fireplaces, where life goes on as it did three generations ago.

Somewhere in the neighbourhood of these old farm-houses there is sure to be an old village. And here England is seen in its most charming aspect. English towns, especially the large ones, are on the whole unattractive and will very seldom bear comparison with any of the delightful German towns. But the beauty of English village architecture need fear no rival. The villages show that the architectonic genius of the country knows how to build houses that are not only comfortable but that also fit into the frame of the surrounding landscape. Only a few miles off a main motor road it is possible to live a fairy-tale life. Black and white houses of the Tudor period are to be seen, or little gems in brick, especially in the south; the north uses grey stone. Then the church with a low, square tower, an old inn with a mediæval sign, and somewhere or other a little collection of thatched roofs. The whole place will be meticulously clean and unspoilt. Owing to the peculiarities of English land tenure very often the whole village belongs to the owner of a great estate whose pride it is not to allow "his" village to be spoilt by tasteless modern innovation.

These are the surroundings and the neighbourhood in which the Englishman feels really at home. It is here that the dreams of the officer in the Indian army are centred, of the civil servant ruling over wild tribes on the equator, of the City man carrying on his business in a dark London office. Once he has made enough money, he will settle down in the country, grow flowers, take the dogs for walks, and play golf. He need never complain of loneliness. His own and his family's friends will be delighted to come and spend the week-end with him. These country houses form the basis of the English week-end, which is unthinkable without them. And for this reason the week-end system cannot be adopted wholesale by other countries. Reciprocally, families living in the country can always reckon on their week-end visitors to put a room at their disposal in London. Thus there is much coming and going between town and country even for people of limited incomes. Above all, girls are by no means cut off from social life by living in the country. They will always find a friend to put them up for the night if they are invited to a dance in London.

Country hospitality is one of the best things that England has to give. Living with one's friends in this way leads to an intimacy which is hard to achieve in a town. Hence anyone who wishes really to get to know the English should visit them in the country. Such a week-end is most restful, its days spent in walking or lazing in the garden, bathing in the neighbourhood, dancing to the gramophone, playing bridge or tennis. Tennis courts are no luxury; nearly every country house has one, and on the larger estates they are a matter of course. Even nowadays England reckons hundreds upon hundreds of country mansions of all sizes up to those that can house thirty guests at a time. Here the well-to-do Englishman lives in the style he likes best, here he carries on his amusements and his love-affairs, here political threads are spun that may have untold consequences. A hierarchy of servants with the butler at its head ensures that every guest is made as comfortable as if he were staying at the Ritz—and in very much pleasanter surroundings. Generations of cultured people have collected the pictures hanging on the walls, among which Van Dycks, Gainsboroughs, and Watteaus are not uncommon, as also the magnificent old silver and china. The proudest German castle is plain in comparison with the treasures to be found in the great English houses, such as Knole, Wilton, Blenheim, and the rest. Nevertheless, the great days of English country houses are numbered, and those who were living in the days of Victoria look back sadly to the good old times. Death duties, financial crises, and the bad state of agriculture have made it necessary for people to "retrench," to sell their Old Masters. Estates have changed hands, passing from the possession of the older families to the new. All this is less surprising than the fact that English country life still survives in a form reminiscent rather of the eighteenth century than of our own day. It may be an anachronism; but it is a part of England, and its passing would leave the country the poorer.

In a previous chapter mention was made of the fact that the owners of huge estates make money in the City to enable them to live the life of a *grand seigneur* in the country. No one whose income is dependent upon agriculture can live that life. Nevertheless, the estates are of an astonishing size and comprise not only land but whole villages in which every house belongs to the landowner. The owner never thinks of farming all his land himself but probably contents himself with the home farm that supplies him with its produce. The remainder is let. The leasehold system is the foundation of English agricultural life. The landlord's chief duty is to keep the premises of his tenants in repair and, when necessary, to finance the harvest. The richer the landlord, the better off are the tenants, who are well aware that it is not their rents which make the landlord rich. Since the prices of agricultural produce suffer by competition with those of the colonies, rents are also low, so that very often great estates yield no more than the amount of the taxes and the sums necessary for keeping the buildings in repair.

Leasehold property exists in every size from great estates down to small farms. The survival of the system is to be explained by the fact that the passing of the lease from father to son has led to a kind of hereditary tenancy; by the English landlord's strong sense of responsibility; and, finally, by the fact that the ideal of possessing one's own plot of land is very much less developed in England than in Germany. If an English farmer has to choose between a good tenancy and a meagre property of his own, he will always decide in favour of the former. Thus England's agricultural problem is not that of turning tenants into owners, but of making agriculture profitable. So long as he is doing well the English farmer is not concerned about the ownership of the land. Hence farmers have not grown more satisfied by the shifting of the balance between leasehold and freehold in favour of the latter as a result of breaking up of great estates. The tendency now is towards the increase of small freehold properties, of which there have always been a good number in

England. This would doubtless be a sign of returning prosperity if at the same time marketing conditions were improving. The fact that this is taking place only to a very limited extent is England's great agrarian difficulty.

The cry is heard throughout England that the land is dying. And anyone who travels through the countryside will realize the truth of it. The train passes for miles through uninhabited districts where much of the land consists of the finest soil, that would support thousands of people in Germany or Italy. In England it forms pasturage for cattle and sheep. It is true that stock-farming plays a great part in a country which has grass incomparably better than any other in Europe and the inhabitants of which have always had a great reputation as breeders of stock. There would, therefore, be nothing to be said against stock-raising if it stood in a proper relationship to the tillage of the soil. But the amount of land under cultivation grows less year by year, with the result that hardly an agricultural report is to be read that does not contain the tragic remark that another so-and-so many acres have "gone out of cultivation." And every acre that is left fallow or turned to grass means the emigration of so many more old farming families to the over-populated towns to swell the ranks of the industrial proletariat.

The blame for this condition of affairs must be laid on the repeal of the Corn Laws in the thirties of the last century. At that time England turned itself from an agrarian into an industrial state and went through the greatest economic revolution in its history. England made this change in order to import cheap foodstuffs from overseas and to sell expensive manufactured goods to other countries which were generations behind her industrially. The result was the immense wealth of the Victorian age, and with it a reconstitution of society whereby the new manufacturer took the place of the old squire, and the urban worker that of the farm labourer. Hideous towns, which are still an affliction to England, grew up like mushrooms, while the countryside began to serve more and more as a luxury dwelling place for the rich. These were the surroundings in which Karl Marx wrote his "Kapital," which has therefore never been applicable in the same degree to Germany as to the country of early capitalism that was in Marx's mind. When Germany entered the ranks of capitalist states, industrialism was already past its worst period. Hence no industrial hell of the English type ever came into being in Germany, bad as things may have been there. Germany may have made less money, because it started later, but it never sinned against its people and its land in the way in which the English Victorian industrialist did. And when Bismarck introduced national health insurance, which was not done in England until Lloyd George's time, there could be no doubt but that Germany had left its rich cousin far behind in social matters. It was only a little while before the War, and under pressure from the new Labour Party, that England's conscience began to stir. Since then, it is only fair to add, enormous progress has been made. Nevertheless, the devastation caused by early English industrialism was too great to be compensated for within a decade or two. It would be an insult to the Ruhr district to put it on a level with many districts in Wales, Scotland, or the Midlands. It is hard to imagine what these places are like. There are endless rows of houses, all exactly similar, each as dirty and damp as the rest. The fogginess of the atmosphere holds the smoke like a pall over the town, so that a few hours' sunshine and blue sky seem like a gala illumination. In London, finally, the dearness of ground rents leads to terrible overcrowding in the poorer districts, the inhabitants of which cannot even escape into the open air. Every visitor to London can have a foretaste from the windows of the railway carriage of the appalling conditions existing in the outskirts of the world's proudest capital. Nor are the slums confined to London; they are to be found in most of the great industrial towns. And as is so often the case, to the evil of poverty is added the evil of alcoholism.

If the brewers and distillers at least gave their customers pleasant surroundings their sins would be less. But the inn, the English equivalent of the German *Wirtshaus*, of the French *estaminet*, of the Italian *osteria*, only exists in the country and in some of the country towns. In the large industrial cities its place has been taken by the "pub," where the customers stand at the bar and consume as much alcohol as they can pay for. There are no tables for eating snacks or playing cards; no kindly landlady to mix with the customers and share their joys and sorrows. That would make the pace much too slow for the beer and whisky lords who control the pubs. Their tenants and employees stand behind the bar, serve drinks out of mechanical containers, and make sure that no one stands at the bar except for so long as he is drinking. Space beside the bar is valuable and must be exploited to the full.

These alcohol and tobacco hells are the meeting-places of the masses of those who have no real home to go to when they return from work. Shilling bets are made on horses and greyhounds, whereby the poor man continually hopes to make his fortune. Hastily swallowed drinks confuse the heads of women as well as men, while children are left waiting at the doors until closing time. As often as not their mothers come out in such a state that they are hardly fit to take them home. Not only women in the West End, but also the poorer class women from the East End drink more than is good for them, and intoxicated women are by no means a rare sight. Anyone who wants to get to know England at its worst may see it in the "pubs." Only one sight is more distressing—the unemployed districts.

There are mining villages in England and whole rows of streets in industrial towns in which men have been unemployed for ten years. These are the "distressed areas," for which King Edward VIII had such profound sympathy. The surprising thing is the demeanour of the inhabitants of these parts. There are neither rioting nor fighting nor revolutionary processions. Want and hope-lessness have so sapped the energies of these unhappy beings that they do nothing but stand about at street corners, smoking cigarettes, making penny bets, and planning visits to the cinema. If ever there was a city of the dead on earth it is here, where pale, emaciated humanity has given up even the hope of better times. Once in a while a few hundreds of them undertake a hunger march to London, where they are permitted to watch the King's arrival to open Parliament. This exhausts their revolutionary energy. When they return home they stand about again at the same street corners and sink back into the same lethargy of hopelessness. The motherland cannot provide them with work. The Dominions need strong young farm labourers and skilled technical workers, and not half-starved, elderly unemployed men and women from the textile and mining industries, or unskilled workers of which England has so vast a superfluity. It is the tragedy of the emigration policy that the kind of man needed overseas is the one who can do equally well in England, while those whom England would gladly spare are of no use to the Dominions either. Up to the present no way has been found out of this dilemma. And it is a very serious one. It must not be forgotten that England cannot issue orders to its Dominions, and that the gigantic self-governing republics of the Empire like Canada, Australia, South Africa, and New Zealand control their own immigration and are by no means disposed to make sacrifices for the sake of the mother country. It is another question whether England might not find room for the unemployed in the Crown colonies in the same way that Mussolini is colonizing the Italian overseas possessions. A little less democracy and more governmental authority might perhaps suggest fresh possibilities. But since England's experience with democracy has been so satisfactory both at home and overseas, it is at least understandable why it should be chary of changing that policy. Instead, it prefers to protect its unemployed from starvation by unemployment relief, and to create fresh opportunities for work by teaching new trades, by starting industries in new places, and by increasing sales. Once again this conservative land is determined to exhaust all the old methods before trying new ones.

Social conditions in England have not been glossed over here. At the same time care must be taken not to paint the picture in unduly sombre colours. A fully skilled worker in permanent employment has nothing to complain of. Moreover, England has made great efforts to improve one of the worst of the post-War social ills—the housing shortage—by building three million new houses. Gradually the slum districts that are a disgrace to the Empire are disappearing, and over-crowding, the most serious effect of the housing shortage, is being diminished. At the same time steps are being taken to strengthen the coming generation for its struggle with life by medical inspection and free milk at school. England is beginning to realize that it cannot gamble with its human material without danger to the security of the empire. The worst reactionaries were shocked when a commission under Sir J. Orr arrived at the conclusion that fifty per cent. of the English nation must from a medical point of view be regarded as under-nourished. The results of this condition and of the increasing urbanization of the English population may be observed by simply passing through some of the poorer quarters, where the people in the streets will all at once be seen to be much shorter than in the West End. This shows that England has not been industrialized for five generations with impunity. At the same time the poorest classes are the most prolific, while better-off people, among whom birth-control is increasingly practised, generally have no more than two or three children. It has been calculated that, unless England's birth-rate goes up, 1935 will have been the peak year of its population, which will be decreasing from then onwards. While England has been coming to this conclusion, the Dominions have been beginning to demand immigrants—though not industrial proletarians—to fill their immense empty spaces after the settlement of the raw materials crisis. Thus England, which a few years ago was looking upon birth-control as the means of curing unemployment, is beginning now to ask itself whether after three or four decades its population will not be too small rather than too large. If the Dominions cannot get enough immigrants of the required type, they will seek them from other nations. And then the question will arise as to the future of the Empire from the British point of view.

Hence England is now beginning to be anxious for the increase of its population both quantitatively and qualitatively. Wealth is taking revenge on those who brought it into existence. Military are added to eugenic considerations. The more seriously England regards the political future of Europe, the more grave must be its own apprehensions. It is known to-day that had the means of defence not kept pace with the submarine offensive during the War England could have been starved out in less than three months. Hence military considerations make it necessary for England to stop the decay of its agriculture. If the question were simply one of the farming class, agriculture might yet be saved. For although southern England, where the villages make a living out of tea-rooms, petrol stations, and golf links, is rapidly losing its farming population, the rest of the country can still produce splendid farm labourers. If only the opportunities for money-making were better, there would still be plenty of hands to do the work, even if the English farmer's wife is more luxurious in her ideas than the German or French. Hardly any women work in the fields in England, for example, and the farmer's daughters who live near a town are only too ready to make for "civilization" and silk stockings. It is necessary to go into the depths of the country to find a sturdy wench bursting with health.

Nevertheless, the agrarian problem is in the main economic. England cannot sell its finished goods in the Dominions if they cannot sell their foodstuffs in the English market. No amount of Ottawa Conventions and preferential tariffs can alter this fact, even if in certain respects they have increased Empire trade. But while the Victorian did not hesitate to sacrifice the farmer in order to pay the industrial worker, modern England realizes the danger of this policy. Hence efforts are being made to save the farmer by subsidizing wheat, by import quotas, fixed prices, and the formation of buying and selling associations. Furthermore, attempts are in progress to make village life more attractive by means of travelling motor cinemas, the modern form of the itinerant circus, and travelling libraries. Amateur dramatic performances, for which all the English, including the country people, have a great love and marked talents, are also encouraged. Given the presence of an energetic teacher, or clergyman, or landowner, no village is so small but that it can give one evening a week to theatricals during the winter months. Nor are any villages without their football and cricket teams, and there is hardly a house without its wireless set. Finally, agricultural shows in villages and market towns tend to enliven country life. Such affairs play a much larger part in England than in Germany, because every Englishman is by nature a stock-breeder, and nothing gives him greater pleasure than to have his horses, cattle, sheep, or sheep-dogs win prizes. England is in the first rank among breeders, with the result that in this respect at all events the farmer may hope to achieve a good return for his labour.

In the so-called hunting counties country life is still further enlivened by fox hunting, which, wherever farming conditions permit of it, has taken on the character of a national sport. Fox hunting is not an exclusive sport. Even though it is primarily dependent on the wealthier classes, anyone can join in who has a horse. The landowner and his tenants and the local farmers all meet on equal terms. Hence class distinctions tend to disappear. Each hunt gives its annual hunt ball. This is the biggest social event in the county, and also a most picturesque one, because on this occasion pink hunting coats are worn instead of the usual tail-coat. Hunting is not only important from the sporting point of view. Its existence is the reason why English horse-breeders are still able to do good business. If to this be added the considerable sums that are paid for damage done to fields and meadows, it will be understood why hunting, despite its feudal character, is not unpopular among the people. Even the societies for the protection of animals meet with no response when they try to protect the fox. They might fare better if the women were on their side. But, unfortunately for the fox, women are no less passionate addicts of hunting than men, despite the dangers connected with this break-neck sport.

Thus the English countryside presents a curious picture. Agriculture is in serious difficulties, but life in the country is as flourishing as ever. The farmers are emigrating, but the townsfolk are immigrating, even if it is only for the few weeks' country life that every Englishman who can possibly afford it regards as his birthright. This is made easier by the English custom of letting fully furnished houses during the summer months by private persons. If a country gentleman is going away, he will let his house for a year or a few weeks, as will also the urban dweller. In the holiday season especially, such good rents can be obtained for houses in country districts that the owners are able to live rent free for the rest of the year. Country holidays are considered even more essential for children than for adults. Efforts are made to provide these not only in the summer but also for the Christmas holidays and especially at Christmas time itself.

No one who has spent Christmas in the country, whether with friends or in his own house, will ever forget the magic of it. This is the real old England, with the venerable habits and customs that have made Christmas the Englishman's greatest festival. But the English Christmas must not be compared with the German. Christmas bells have a fundamentally different tone in the two countries.

The German bells are the voice of the cathedral, a grave reminder of the greatest event in the history of the world, and the solemnity of its character never permits any riotousness, despite the joyousness of the children. The popping of champagne corks and crackers simply do not fit in with a German Christmas, just as they are inseparable from an English one. In England Christmas is a day of rejoicing, as if it were the King's birthday or the nation had won a great victory. The religious motif is only felt in the background, and then only the remembrance of Bethlehem. The memory of the fact that the path which began there ended upon Golgotha is overlaid on this day by the commandment: "Rejoice!"

The English Christmas is as different from the German in its outward manifestation as in character. Christmas Eve is not the culminating point, with the lighting of the Christmas tree and the distribution of presents. In fact, Christmas Eve in the German sense does not exist at all. Its place is taken by the Christmas stocking, breakfast on Christmas morning, and in the afternoon, entirely separate from the rest of the festivities, a lighted-up Christmas tree. Christmas to the English child means December 25th, not December 24th, though it begins at six or seven o'clock in the morning. During the night of December 24th to 25th, Father Christmas makes his rounds, flying through the air on a sleigh drawn by reindeer and descending the chimney to fill the stocking, borrowed from the largest member of the family, that every English child hangs on the end of its bed during this eventful night.

The presents that Father Christmas puts into the stocking are only the smallest of his gifts, apples and nuts, little wooden toys, pencils, and tiny dolls. The real Christmas presents that have been put "on order" after weighty consideration and which would not fit into the largest stocking ever made, are to be found on the breakfast table. They are all carefully wrapped up in paper, red or green, Father Christmas' heraldic colours, and decorated with holly and twigs of fir as an indication of joys to come. While bacon and eggs wait in vain for consumption, and half-empty teacups get mixed up with string and sealing wax, the breakfast room turns into a welter of red paper, green ribbons, fir twigs, boxes, pieces of cardboard, and unread letters and postcards.

The same pace is kept up throughout the day until the Christmas tree is lit up after tea. At tea itself there is the inevitable Christmas cake, upon which the cook has worked so hard that it can only be digested with the help of bicarbonate of soda—a medicine inseparable from the idea of Christmas. Then at last the Christmas tree comes into its own; though Germanic in origin, it is now customary in all parts of England. The mistletoe bough, that used to play such an important part in Victorian days, now hangs under the chandelier, a half bankrupt competitor. Nowadays England's young men and maidens no longer need the mistletoe. It is their grandmothers who refuse to abandon it.

Unless people prefer to serve the ritual turkey and mince-pies of the English Christmas at lunch time, dinner is the real function of the day. Once again there is a difference between England and Germany. In Germany Christmas is a festivity restricted to the immediate family. The English invite any solitary friends to dinner in order that they may not be lonely and joyless on this day of days. Hence the company that takes its place round the table gay with red crackers and holly is likely to be a numerous one in the larger houses. The dining-room is a sea of light and colours until towards the end of the meal the lights are turned out while the blazing plum pudding makes its entry. This *chef d'œuvre* of English culinary art, which in its simplest form contains twenty-four ingredients, has been in the making for months in advance. The ceremony of stirring the plum pudding takes place six weeks before Christmas.

Thus tradition does after all spread a gleam of reverence over what is perhaps a shade too noisy a feast for German ideas. This is especially true of country districts, where England's ancient Christmas carols are sung in the village streets, and the squire gives presents in a truly patriarchal fashion to every employee down to the humblest gardener's boy. This giving of presents (which is extended to all poor people) to friends and relations to the tenth degree is more than a mere question of money. It is a matter of kindness of heart, and a manifestation of one of the best characteristics of the English—their desire to help. The birth of the Saviour is an occasion for rejoicing, and this joy is expressed in an almost naïve form by eating and drinking, singing and dancing. But since Christ preached "Love thy neighbour," presents are given with open hands in order that honour may be done the Master in this fashion. This is a Christmas spirit that has not died out in the country which, despite gala nights in the big hotels and over-indulgence in gramophone and wireless music, can boast of having produced the loveliest

Christmas story in the world in Dickens' "Christmas Carol."

Christmas in the country is England's most beautiful Christmas, just as life in the country is England's most delightful form of life. Country life, that at the turn of the century was the prerogative of a relatively small number of town dwellers, is now coming to be progressively more of general benefit. With the hiking movement, founded on the German *Wandervogel*, the youth of England has found its way back to Nature. Every year in the summer time English meadows are covered with white tents, in which the young wanderers spend their nights, while caravans attached to motor cars provide cheap accommodation for thousands of families. Moreover, the whole of England is covered with a network of motor buses which, while they certainly disturb the peace and beauty of the countryside, give the broad masses of the town dwellers a chance of getting out into the fresh air. The tourist traffic in country districts has been increasing ever since the devaluation of the pound made foreign travel more expensive. The Englishman suddenly discovered how much there is to be seen in his own island. So did the foreigner, who had until then confined his visits to London and its neighbourhood, and who has now all at once begun to appear in the fine old cathedral cities like York, Exeter, Winchester, Wells, and the rest. And nobody—unless he is rained upon in torrents— will regret a visit to Wales, Scotland, or the Hebrides, where Nature speaks in grander tones than in the somewhat tame and orderly southern counties of England. It is just as mistaken to take Surrey and Sussex and the

93

watering places on the south coast as typical of the whole of England as it is to judge the English by the Victorian standard of culture of the middle classes. England is richer both in scenery and people than they think who have only known the hackneyed counties and the average Englishman.

CHAPTER VI

STATE, POLITICS, AND PRESS

THE King is the head of the British State. He is a constitutional monarch bound to accept the advice of Parliament and his Ministers. Nevertheless, although these latter are the actual rulers of the country, it is a mistake to call the King a mere figurehead. This could only be true if an English monarch happened to be personally ineffectual. If, on the other hand, the King is an able man, his position gives him every opportunity of playing his part in the work of government. In case of conflict the sovereign is obliged to yield to Parliament, as Queen Victoria and Edward VIII found to their sorrow. Edward VII and his son, on the other hand, always made it their sedulous endeavour to avoid any difference of opinion with the Government, which actually strengthened the influence of the Crown. England is one of the few present-day countries in which the power of the Crown has increased. This is especially the result of the Statute of Westminster in 1931, which turned the Dominions practically into independent republics with the Crown as the connecting link. The loyalty to the Crown of England's overseas possessions and of the Dominions, where the Governor-General carries out the functions of the King, is indeed remarkable, and is one of the reasons why the mother country clings so firmly to the monarchical system. Even the most radical of English politicians, who would gladly overthrow the existing economic and social order, stop short at the Crown. They realize the advantages it confers upon England and the Empire.

As in the case of so many English institutions, the rights and duties of the Crown have been defined in the course of centuries. It has become customary for the King to seek out some particular sphere of activity for which he is specially gifted in addition to his general representational and governmental duties. Thus Edward VII was his country's foreign minister, while George V distinguished himself more especially in internal politics, as, for instance, at the time of the creation of the National Government, when he induced Baldwin and Macdonald to serve in the same Cabinet. It was Edward VIII's ambition, on the other hand, to be the social worker among the monarchs of England, which explains his great popularity among the working classes. The fact that he was nevertheless obliged to abdicate proves the power of the middle classes and the Church, for whom in this case Mr. Baldwin acted as spokesman.

Thus the functions of the King of England are somewhat elastic. His position is greater or less according to his personal influence. But if ever a king should throw away the Crown, no one would be sorrier than the English themselves, who are in their heart of hearts a monarchical people. England loves the Court with its picturesque mediæval ceremonial. All London runs to see the King drive to the opening of Parliament in his golden coach with an escort of Guards in order to read the speech from the throne to the purple and ermine-clad

Lords and their be-jewelled Ladies. Similarly, George V's jubilee was a national festival in the best sense of the word, as also has been the coronation of his son. At such times, when all nations meet together in London, England feels itself to be the centre of the world and the greatest empire in history. It knows the propaganda value of such occasions, quite apart from the fact that a coronation or jubilee Season means an immense amount of business for the metropolis.

While the English people bestow an honest affection upon their royal house, they also demand a great deal from it. The life of the King of England and of his family is not an easy one. England expects its royal family to be continually in evidence and, over and above its London duties, not to neglect the provinces nor the Empire. The series of inaugurations of buildings and exhibitions, investitures, parades, sporting and Court functions is only broken by the extremely important visits to the Dominions. In addition to representational duties there are the more definitely governmental functions, such as the summons to a Party leader to form a Cabinet, holding meetings of the Privy Council, the opening of Parliament, or the signing of State documents. Before receiving the King's assent all laws have previously passed through the two Houses which form the foundation of the British Constitution. These do not actually divide the legislative function equally between them, since the Upper House only has the right to delay a measure for two years, and this only so long as it is not concerned with finance. In practice this means that a bill which has passed the third reading in the

House of Commons may be modified in detail by the House of Lords, but in its main outlines will keep the form given it in the Lower House. If the Upper House should prove obdurate, the Government can threaten it with the creation of a large number of peers who will ensure the requisite majority in the House of Lords. With admirable common sense, the Lords never let things go so far. They realize that a hereditary Upper House is an anachronism which may bring its own suppression upon itself if it should enter into competition with the House chosen by the people's will. For this reason, too, all attempts to reform the Upper House have failed. The less the gilded House of Lords is tampered with the better.

The real function of the Upper House consists in providing a non-combative atmosphere in which the measures that have passed the Lower House may be debated anew. This frequently is intolerably wearisome. On great occasions, however, the House of Lords becomes as it were a Roman Senate where England's elder statesmen and the political wisdom of centuries are able to serve their country afresh. A debate in which Grey, Birkenhead, Asquith, Balfour, and Haldane spoke must have been unequalled in the world. All these men had a long career of statesmanship and politics behind them before they passed into the limpid placidity of the House of Lords, where their experience could once again be used for the benefit of their native land.

While membership of the Upper House makes an excellent end, it is a bad beginning to a political career. Indeed, it is a handicap to an ambitious young politician to be a member of the House of Lords. The spurs of high politics are won in the House of Commons, which can only be entered after a stern electioneering fight. Hence the English Member of Parliament sets the letters M.P. after his name with great pride. And England looks with pride at its House of Commons, in front of which stands the figure of Cromwell, the man who signed the death warrant of absolutism. There is a curious atmosphere about the Parliament buildings— the House of Commons on the left and the House of Lords on the right. The neogothic architecture is, with the exception of the old banqueting hall, as second-rate as the numberless statues of English statesmen erected here and the pictures representing scenes from English history. A sensation of awe nevertheless overcomes the visitor, who feels himself to be in the high temple of history. History is here so mighty that it over-shadows æsthetics. The chairmen of the two Houses —the Speaker in the Commons and the Lord Chancellor in the Lords—carry out their functions fitly attired in wig and gown. On the other hand, the practice of Members of Parliament of wearing a top hat during sessions, which was formerly invariable, is dying out. More recently Sir Austen Chamberlain was almost the only man in the House of Commons who carried on the old tradition.

While continental Houses of Parliament are built in horseshoe shape, it is due to England's ancient two-Party system that at Westminster the members sit in rows opposite one another, with the Speaker at the upper end. It is thus possible to tell at a glance the strength of both the Government and the Opposition. The Government always sits on the front bench of the seats occupied by the Party in power, so that the English Parliament has no Government table but simply a "front bench." This shows in graphic form that government in England is by Party, as well as the fact that no one can be a member of the Government who is not a member of one or other of the Houses. Hence the leader of the majority Party is England's Prime Minister. After a General Election the King calls upon him to form a Cabinet, whether he happens to have the King's confidence or not. It is well known how much Queen Victoria disliked being forced to summon Gladstone to form a Government. Nevertheless, she was obliged, willy-nilly, to do so. More important than the confidence of the monarch is the confidence of the Party, without which no Government can remain in power, since the Party can at any time overthrow the Government. For this reason the annual Party congresses at which the leaders of the Government and Opposition justify their policy to their followers are of great importance, even though they commonly end with the triumph of Party discipline over grumblers and critics.

Discipline is one of the chief reasons for the success of the parliamentary system in England. It prescribed the suppression of private differences for the sake of the Party and was responsible for the fact that for centuries England was governed by the two-Party system, to which it seems to be returning now that the Liberal Party has faded away. Even in these days when antagonism between the Conservative and Labour Parties is growing more acute, the House of Commons has reason to be proud of its self-control. This is due not least to the peculiar style of debate which the House has

developed in the course of its history. If a member
wishes to make a thunderous appeal to the nation, to
appear as a world reformer, or to incite his followers to
class warfare, he does it outside at Party or election
meetings. In the House itself he adopts the traditional
style which prescribes the use of a conversational tone.
In order to impress the Lower House a speaker must
speak coolly and objectively. He must not exaggerate
or pour forth denunciations of his adversaries. Shouting,
abuse, and gesticulation are not merely penalized but are
quite ineffectual. And a speaker must never read his
speech. It would indeed be a risky proceeding in a
House where interruptions play so large a part in
debate and whose members enjoy nothing so much as
repartee. A good riposte may be more effective than the
longest speech. Moreover, the manner in which the
House ignores the results of chance divisions unfavourable to the Government that would lead to a ministerial
crisis in France is admirable. The *genius loci* of Westminster seems to keep watch to ensure that however
high political feelings may run, their vocal expression
shall be kept within bounds. All England was shocked
when a left-radical member permitted himself as a joke
to wave in the air the golden mace that lies in front of
the Speaker. It was a piece of bad form which even the
culprit's friends did not condone.

The discipline enforced by the Lower House on its
members is the more remarkable because wild scenes
often occur outside Westminster, especially at election
times, when the waves of political passion run high and
every conceivable method of propaganda is used. An
election battle in England may take on the appearance of

a popular festival, with processions, banners, bands, aeroplanes, motor cars, loud-speakers, posters, and leaflets. Every voter, that is to say all men and women over the age of twenty-one, must be canvassed. This is made the easier because electoral districts are small and members who enter Parliament with a majority of only a few dozen votes are not uncommon. Whoever obtains a simple majority of votes is elected. The votes of the other Parties are lost. England has no system of proportional representation which makes for justice, but neglects the voter's personal interest in his candidate. And it is a question which is the more important—to have a Parliament which represents public opinion with mathematical exactness, or one in which the voter, at any rate at the time of the elections, takes a passionate interest? In this case the worse system is the better. While recognizing the unfairness of its electoral system, England is more than chary of altering it.

The English voter gives his vote primarily for a particular individual. Secondarily, for some special question which has been chosen as the electioneering slogan by the Party authorities. Hence votes are not only given for the Socialist Party or the Conservative, but for or against Protection, or rearmament, or the Zinovieff letter, or hanging the Kaiser, or whatever the cry of the moment happens to be. A good election slogan, however foolish it may be, may therefore determine the fate of the House of Commons. The English political tactician thus takes into account the fact that the English are on the whole not specially interested in Party politics as such. The number of people who can be reckoned upon to vote regularly for one Party is relatively small, and at every election it is the so-called floating vote which is decisive. Mr. Smith may call himself a Liberal and may have voted for that Party for years. This will not prevent his voting Conservative if this Party happens to choose an election slogan that appeals to him. At the next elections he may return to the Liberal fold or vote Labour for a change. It is always the momentary situation, not Party ideals, which influences him in casting his vote. This is the reason why the results of English elections are so hard to predict, with the further result that betting on the elections has become a national sport. Enormous sums may be lost or won after an unexpected election result.

Whatever may be the faults of the English electoral system in practice and however much may be said against the House of Commons, both have the advantage of being absolutely suited to the English people. Nothing would be more fatal than to try to transfer bodily a purely English system to countries which have none of the English characteristics. First of all Eton and Oxford would have to be created, then the "gentleman" type must be bred, compromise must be raised to the level of an ideal, millions must be inoculated with the capacity for scenting danger from afar, a wide and well-to-do middle class must be brought into being, a few centuries' political training and history must be added—and then—and then only—the soil would be ready for planting parliamentary institutions after the English model. Anything else is bound to lead to parody.

The work done at Westminster and by the Privy Council is only a part of English government. There are in addition the Ministries and self-governing bodies, and besides Members of Parliament there are the Civil Servants. It is one of the peculiarities of English social life that, apart from the Foreign Office, the Civil Service should play so negligible a rôle in society. England can show nothing to compare with the position held by the higher administrative officials in German social life. In England it seems as if gnomes must do the work of the district and urban councils, so little do their members come into the light of day. Any that do become visible, like the Sheriff or the Lord Lieutenant of a county, have honorary functions that are of so ceremonial a nature that they can hardly be called official. Nor is there any official form of address. They remain plain Mr. So-and-so all their lives.

Like everything else in England, there is an historical explanation for the position of the Civil Servants. English administration is based on the principle of self-government and upon a number of special privileges gained in the course of its history. As a result, the English administrative apparatus is a structural monstrosity. Everything is most uneconomical and illogical. Nor is the central office, the Home Office in London, a Ministry of the Interior in the German sense, but a kind of Ministry of Police, controlling the police, the sale of poisons, the protection of children, immigration, and similar matters. The title of Ministry of the Interior might with greater propriety be claimed by the Ministry of Health, although even here the parallel with Germany is not complete. It is true that the officials of the Ministry of Health, like those of the other government offices, are government officials. These are almost the only government officials in the English administration.

The remaining officials, who work in the provinces, are appointed by the bodies who employ them; that is to say, they are district and provincial officials. County officials are purely a matter for the county itself. Their posts are put up for public competition and are filled as the county thinks best. There are sixty-two such counties in England and Wales and at the head of each is an elected county parliament, the County Council. It is, amongst other things, the duty of this body to provide itself with a permanent staff of officials and especially with a Clerk of the Council. From an administrative point of view this inconspicuous title conceals one of the most powerful men in the county. Besides the Clerk of the Council, who is generally a lawyer, there are the Treasurer, the Officer of Health, who is responsible for public hygiene, the Director of Education, and others, each of whom is attached to a special committee of the County Council. In comparison with these officials, the Lord Lieutenant of the County, who is appointed by the King and is generally one of the great local landowners, and the Sheriff are more or less decorative adjuncts. One of the functions of the Sheriff, for instance, is to receive the judges on circuit as they enter the county. If anyone is condemned to death, he has the ghastly duty of attending the execution.

England would not be England if the whole system proceeded on these simple lines. The sequence is broken by non-county boroughs, as well as urban and rural districts, to the number of some thirteen hundred and fifty, which, while they form part of the county, are in practice independent. Next there are eighty-three county boroughs which have no connection at all with the county. All large cities like Liverpool, Manchester, and Birmingham are "boroughs," a word the definition of which is given up as impossible even by the *Encyclopædia Britannica*. The importance of the boroughs to English administration is the greater since they form the real historical foundation of the self-government of the land.

As a county has its County Council, so a borough has its Town Council, and the Town Clerk corresponds to the Clerk of the Council. His post, again, is more important than might be supposed from the title. The Town Clerk has practically the same position as the German burgomaster. The duties of the English burgomaster—the mayor—are far more representational than in Germany, although at times he may act as a police magistrate ; a statement that is true even of the one best known in the world—the Lord Mayor of London, an office that is not to be confused with that of *Oberbürgermeister* in Berlin. London has twenty-nine mayors, who rule over the twenty-nine Metropolitan boroughs independently of one another. One of these boroughs is the City, whose mayor has the title of Lord Mayor, but who has no jurisdiction beyond the bounds of the City, whereas the *Oberbürgermeister* of Berlin rules all over Berlin.

The fact that the Lord Mayor in reality only rules over the City and not over Greater London in no way detracts from the splendour of his position. On great occasions he is surrounded with mediæval civic magnificence, as when he drives through the City in a golden coach to receive the King at Temple Bar, or gives a banquet at the Guildhall for members of Government and foreign ambassadors, or takes part in the annual costumed procession, the famous Lord Mayor's Show. Before a Lord Mayor reaches this eminence, he must be an alderman, a title also borne by a certain number of the Town and County Councillors. The Lord Mayor holds office for a year. At the end of which time nothing remains to him but his knightly title and an empty purse. Despite the high emoluments of the position, the claims made on the Lord Mayor of London are ruinous.

The immense importance of the system of self-government means that the elections to the Town and County Councils are great political events, in which the whole of England and the House of Commons in particular take a lively interest. For since these elections are fought on more or less Party political lines, their results form a good barometer of the mood of the nation. At present the council elections are the more important, because it is especially in them that the Socialists have made advances, with the result that London has a Socialist majority. Hence there are really two election campaigns in England, one for the House of Commons and one for the Town and County Councils. The Englishman is therefore reminded at every turn of his civic duties. Taken as a whole, the English self-government has contributed very greatly to the development of a civic sense and to inducing the various parts of the country to take part in the management of their own affairs.

On the other hand, it cannot be denied that it produces a local particularism that makes any unification of the administration very much more difficult. Good as English administration may be, there is often friction between the various parts. It was a tremendous step forward for England when it succeeded in centralizing road-making, which had previously been in a state of indescribable chaos. Nor is this surprising when it is remembered how restricted are the powers of the central Ministries. Their function is much more to act as a sort of clearing-house for the towns and counties and to issue suggestions to them. The Board of Education does not draw up a curriculum to be applied to all schools. It simply provides the local and autonomous school authorities with general guiding principles.

The nature of the most difficult problem awaiting solution in England to-day is thus revealed in its administrative system—namely, how to combine the individualism of the English people with the duty of working for the common good. England realizes how much vital force is derived from individualism. But it also realizes that present-day conditions demand a more centralized and powerful type of organization that is lacking to it. Rationalization may seem less picturesque than the governmental system of the past. But it is inevitable in the long run.

If English political life can be reduced to a formula, it is that nothing can be done except what has the expressed or tacit approval of public opinion. From this point of view the British Empire is ruled in precisely the same fashion as a village in Somerset. Ultimately it is not the will of the Government which becomes law, but the will of the people. Hence the Government can undertake nothing without making certain that it possesses the consent of public opinion, which in its turn has the power to oblige the Government and Parliament itself to follow the course it desires. Hence the caution and the slowness of English politics that drive foreigners to distraction. Before taking a single step, the Government must first test the ground of public opinion. Millions must have signified their assent—even if it is only in the form of silence—before the Cabinet can determine its policy. When a really important question of foreign politics arises, the number of millions is increased, because nearly the same procedure that has been gone through in England has to be repeated in the Dominions. The Dominion Governments again can only do what their public opinion permits; and public opinion in the Dominions does not dance to Westminster's piping, especially since the year 1931. At that time the Dominions were turned into what are virtually independent Republics, with the result that the British Empire, which has adopted the for once perfectly logical title of Commonwealth of Nations, is in reality a federation of peoples. Whether or not the Dominions choose to stay in the Empire depends ultimately upon their own wishes, and thus upon the capacity of England to make it worth their while to do so. That this is not merely a form of speech was shown by the case of Southern Ireland, which was with startling frankness given to understand that no hindrance would be put in the way of its resigning its position within the Empire. Only Ireland must realize that in this case it would be treated as a foreign country and the Irish as foreigners. If Dublin severs its connection with London, it will therefore be cut off by tariff walls from the English market, which takes ninety per cent. of its exports, and England will have the right to withdraw the permission to work from hundreds of thousands of Irishmen employed in England. It is obvious why De Valera, even though he has abolished the post of Governor-General, clings to the thread that unites Ireland with the Empire.

Although since the Ottawa Conventions and the resultant preferential tariffs the idea of the economic unity of the empire has been strengthened, the magnetic attraction that England exercises upon its Dominions is not solely due to the economic benefits that accrue. The military unity of the Empire is equally important and takes the form of England's means of defence being placed at the disposal of the Dominions. Australia and New Zealand would be obliged to build immense navies if they wished to permit themselves the luxury of abandoning the Empire, while the Union of South Africa would have to be prepared one day to try conclusions with the negro world all by itself. Thus England's youthful overseas republics can judge by the smallness of their armaments budgets what inclusion within the Empire is worth to them. This, however, does not apply to Canada, which could not be defended in case of attack by America. Sentimental and economic grounds therefore play the chief part in its loyalty.

Canada and Australia, New Zealand, the Union of South Africa, and the Irish Free State have full Dominion status. As such they have their own parliaments and cabinets, while, with the exception of Ireland, the link with the motherland is represented by a Governor-General who is appointed by the King. India, whose

Governor-General is called a Viceroy, has not yet
achieved this position. The unparallelled experiment
is being tried here of making an Asiatic country with
the dimensions of a continent " ripe " for western
democracy. No one can say whether or not the attempt
will be successful. England, therefore, before bestowing
Dominion status upon India, has reserved a number of
military and economic safeguards. In its present tran-
sitional stage India may be called a half Dominion.
The British Empire as a whole must be regarded as a
terraced structure, with the Dominions on the highest
level and the most backward among Crown Colonies,
Protectorates, and Spheres of Interest on the lowest.
In between come colonies which have already achieved
a certain degree of self-government, and sometimes, as
in the case of Rhodesia, a very considerable proportion.
It is and always has been the highest aim of English
policy to educate its overseas territories up to self-
administration, even if this means that they thereby
lose touch with England : a policy that is in the sharpest
possible contrast with the colonial policy of France,
which seeks to make north Africa into a French pro-
vince. England's ambition, on the contrary, is not to be
lord over life and death in the Empire, but to be its
clearing-house. It is a magnificent conception and
unique in the history of the world.

Democracy too has been accorded a free hand. It is
therefore necessary to understand why England clings
so tenaciously to its democratic system, which not only
influences every least part of the government of the
mother country, but upon which the whole Empire is
built up. With the exception of India, which remains

an unsolved problem, England has been fortunate in possessing a governmental system capable of taking root in so many different lands. It is true that England was sowing its seed upon virgin soil, where no traditions existed or where they had died out. Where traditions still existed, as, for example, in India, democracy has still many a hard fight before it.

A straight line runs from the family to school, from school to parish, State, or Empire. Everything is based upon the same principle—that of allowing the individual so much freedom and giving him so much responsibility as are consistent with public welfare. England's highest political precept runs: "Each one for himself and each one for the common weal." Its practice has produced a structure possessing at once remarkable moral strength and an undeniable material vulnerability. If England should fall, it would be a fearful and irreparable catastrophe. A commonwealth of the peculiar type of the British Empire could never come into being again. Of all the possible dangers, England's greatest dread is of war, for every great war is a threat to the life of the Empire. No one knew whether Australia and New Zealand, Canada and South Africa would be prepared to march in August 1914. And what would be the present state of the Empire if one or all of them had stood aside in the hour of desperate need? Since then the independence of the Dominions has been greatly enlarged. Hence in the interests of its Empire and not merely from a commercial point of view, England is bound to be peace-loving. Nor is there any cogent reason against it, since there is nothing left for England to win and much for her to lose. In these circumstances it is easy enough to play the part of the peace-lover ; and moreover very useful. Love of peace and loyalty to the League of Nations are moral signboards of which England cannot have too many in order to educate its overseas territories up to loyalty to the Empire.

Nevertheless, in order to be prepared for all emergencies, peace-loving England is arming at a rate and to a degree never before known in times of peace. But weapons are of no avail unless there are men who are prepared to wield them. A war not sanctioned by public opinion would be a matter of life and death from the moment of its declaration. The men who had bound England to France and Russia lived through some anxious hours in August 1914, until they succeeded in exploiting the German invasion of Belgium as a mobilization slogan. The Government needs the support of public opinion for every important undertaking and not merely for war. It is able to ensure this, just as in its turn public opinion can provide itself with the Government it wants. An example of this occurred in December 1935, when popular indignation at the Hoare-Laval scheme drove the English Secretary of State for Foreign Affairs out of office. There is a sort of interaction between the Government and public opinion by means of which it is from time to time decided which shall take the initiative and which is the stronger.

When the Government wishes to sound or to influence public opinion, it has at its disposal the House of Commons, public meetings in the provinces with addresses by Ministers who spend their time travelling about the country, the wireless, and last but not least the Press. The Press therefore plays a part in England which it never played in Germany. No Government could maintain itself for any length of time against a determinedly hostile Press, nor could it oppose any desires expressed emphatically by the Press. An enormous responsibility rests upon the Press, which is all the greater since the complete freedom of the Press is limited only by the laws of libel and the laws for safeguarding public morality. And the Press watches over this freedom with lynx eyes. Thus England has no official organ that writes at the behest of the Government. Although there are means whereby the Government may influence the Press, the editor always reserves the right to say the last word. This is true even for *The Times*, which is in such close contact with the Government. It is quite capable of saying what it thinks if it is not satisfied with the Government's policy. In such cases *The Times* feels that it stands above the Government, as guardian of public interests. Only a journal of the standing and traditions of *The Times* could make and enforce such a claim, which has created for it a position apart not only in England but in the whole world. It is therefore perfectly safe to take news in *The Times* as authentic until the contrary is shown. Rather than risk being caught out in the publication of an erroneous piece of news, *The Times*, whose pride it is to be the index of world history, prefers to suppress anything that seems of doubtful authenticity. This attitude is not free from a certain academic tinge, and it is therefore not surprising to find that this is not a paper intended for the masses, but for those people who are politically influential.

The next place to that of *The Times* belongs to the

Daily Telegraph, which is also a high-class paper and which fills the gap left by *The Times*. Anyone who wishes to know what happened yesterday reads *The Times*. Those who want to know what may happen to-morrow will take the *Daily Telegraph*, which more nearly resembles a continental newspaper than does the typical English *Times*. While the *Daily Telegraph* contains very sound political speculation, *The Times* hardly ever yields to the temptation to forecast the future. The number of serious journals is increased by the *Morning Post*, an excellently written and well-staffed paper, though its circle of readers is of necessity somewhat limited by its extreme Conservative bias. Furthermore there are the great provincial papers, the *Manchester Guardian*, *Yorkshire Post*, and *Glasgow Herald*, as well as the Sunday papers, *The Sunday Times* and *The Observer*. Since English daily newspapers are not published on Sundays, England provides itself with special Sunday papers, which are not weeklies but daily papers published once a week.

There is a sharp line of demarcation between the high-class Press and the popular Press. The latter, which consists of the *Daily Mail*, *Daily Express*, and of the slightly more serious *News Chronicle* and *Daily Herald*, is intended for a completely different circle of readers from that of the papers mentioned above. These papers cater for the broad masses of the people who do not wish to be instructed so much as entertained, and who seem to be able to endure politics only if they are presented in a setting of murder trials, fires, culinary recipes, sports news, and love-stories. At the same time none of these papers can be said to belong to the category of the "yellow press." On the contrary ; between the most pointless interviews excellent articles are to be found, which these papers are able to afford thanks to their enormous wealth, as also they shun no expense in connection with their reporters and photographic staff. The make-up of the popular Press is excellent, and not to be surpassed for liveness, brevity, and "snap." It forms the Americanized section of the English Press with all the advantages and drawbacks of the system. It has caused millions of Englishmen who would otherwise never look at a paper to become newspaper readers, and has thereby tended to a spread of culture. On the other hand, it has also bred superficiality, a love of sensation, and a morbid interest in accidents and crime. Thanks to its appeal to these instincts, it has succeeded in achieving a circulation which has never been approached by any German newspaper. *Mail* and *Express*, *Chronicle* and *Herald*, are round about the two million mark, whereas in the ranks of the more serious news-sheets the *Daily Telegraph* created a record when its circulation rose to half a million.

The man responsible for this development was Lord Northcliffe, Europe's greatest journalistic genius. He was also, however, responsible for the introduction of the trust system into the newspaper world whereby, in combination with an enormous system of advertising, the Press has made incredible sums of money. This again has led to the concentration of power in a few hands, the dangers of which are undeniable. Northcliffe's brother, Lord Rothermere, the brothers Berry, who to-day sit in the Upper House as Lord Camrose and Lord Kemsley, control networks of newspapers which cover the whole of England and to which a few men may if they so wish dictate their policy. Lord Beaverbrook even made attempts at intervals to turn his papers into a political Party fighting for the British Empire under the banner of Isolation. A curiosity in another sense is the *Daily Herald*, the official organ of the Labour Party, which belongs to the extremely capitalist trust known as Odham's Press, of which nothing would remain should the *Herald* realize its socialistic ideals. A capitalist undertaking financing the anti-capitalist campaign is a phenomenon only possible in England; as is also the case of Low, England's most famous political caricaturist, who every now and then puts his pencil at the service of the Left and even of class-warfare in the *Evening Standard*, which is the property of the capitalist and Conservative Lord Beaverbrook.

No reasonable Englishman would deny that his newspapers at times descend to depths unworthy of the nation to which they belong. No one is safe from being attacked by a mob of reporters, who do not hesitate even at the most personal affairs. Not infrequently the reporter himself is embarrassed when he is sent to interview the mother of a child that has been run over or the brother of a murderer. Not the English journalist, who is a decent, straightforward fellow, is responsible for the excrescences on the Press, but a system which will use almost any means in its hunt for readers and advertisements. Only recently a stand has been made by the newspaper men themselves against these misuses of journalism. Nevertheless, while there are deep shadows, there is also much light. England's best newspapers are the best in the world. And it is they who exert the strongest influence. For in devoting itself to entertainment journalism the popular Press sacrificed its political effectiveness. The Englishman is far too critical a reader of newspapers not to judge a report by the place of its publication ; a statement that is certainly true of people who read more than one newspaper. This is much more customary in England than in Germany. The consumption of newspapers by the Englishman—not forgetting the Englishwoman—is colossal. It begins at breakfast, when the great papers that only appear once a day are laid on the table. For the afternoon and evening there are the evening papers that are independent journals and not second editions of the morning papers. Then there are the Sunday papers, periodicals, magazines, technical papers, sports papers, and society papers which tell of the life and doings of Society. Provision is indeed made for every taste.

The life of England resembles an immense piece of dough that is daily kneaded by the hands of thousands of journalists. Every side of English life is reflected in the newspaper columns. The most widely separate elements in the country are brought into contact with one another by reading about each other. At the same time the newspapers provide a sure means of appeal to every English heart. In times of crisis the Government has only to ensure itself of the co-operation of a handful of newspaper proprietors in order to weld together the English nation into a solid *bloc*. The World War showed what a terrible weapon the Press could be in English hands both at home and wherever English is read and spoken. No country in the world possesses a journalistic medium that will stand comparison with the English for power and success in propaganda. It acts not only by means of the written word but equally forcefully through illustrations and caricatures. The times are long past when England made mock of its illustrated papers, saying they were intended for people who could not read. Nowadays illustrations form a part of every paper, from *The Times* downwards.

It is impossible to understand English democracy unless the Press is given its proper place. The Press is a far more popularly representative organ than the wireless, and increases the power of the Government, which, with the help of the newspapers, is able to loose the storms of moral indignation without which the broad masses of the English people cannot be induced to rouse themselves to action. The Englishman will only fight if he thinks he is fighting for a great ideal. The fact that these ideals always seem to coincide with the personal interests of England is England's good fortune, and due to its own cleverness as well as that of its Press. Moral or immoral, the Press serves England, its power and its glory—a service that surely atones for many vices.

CHAPTER VII

CHURCH AND LAW

NO one can understand England who considers only politics and business, sport and amusement, and overlooks the part played by the Church in the life of the people. Religion may be more intensive in Scotland and Wales than in England proper, perhaps it pulses more vividly in the Nonconformist than in the Established Church. These are only differences of degree, which do not alter the fact that the English nation is definitely church-going. In the first place this is due to the predominance of morality in the English character. Even when he is doubtful of the dogma of Christianity, the Englishman accepts its ethics, and regards it as the best of all systems of morality. Secondly, the Englishman is religious by tradition. For centuries England has lived under the threefold banner of Crown, Parliament, and Church, and experience has shown that it has not fared too badly under this ensign. Why, therefore, interfere with the things that have made it great? So the Englishman as a matter of course pays his tribute to the Church, just as he stands up for "God Save the King", without greatly troubling as to whether he is a convinced monarchist or a true Christian. The habit of deep soul-searching is not the Englishman's strong point, but neither is it his weakness—a weakness that has led many a man to an empty void instead of to glorious certainty.

It may therefore be said that the Englishman stands in a relationship to his Church—or more accurately, to his Churches—similar to that in which he stands to his State. Is not England, in the words of the old joke, a country of a hundred religions and only one sauce? This is still true. England can show far greater religious differences than other European countries, whose alternatives are simply Catholic and Protestant. In England there are at least three main groups—the Established Church, the Free Churches, and the Church of Rome. These, however, are only the most general divisions, as the first two sections are subdivided into a medley of lesser divisions. Thus the Established Church, the Church of England, is divided into the Anglo-Catholic and the Evangelical, or in the current phrase, High and Low Church. Both are Protestant in the sense of dogma, though they have taken over the episcopal organization and part of the rites of Roman Catholicism. The High Church with its Masses and confessions differs very little from the Roman cult, while the Low Church approaches more nearly Continental Protestantism. Nevertheless, High and Low Church are not separate religious sects but are different tendencies within the same community. At the same time the differences are indeed so acute that a Bishop of Low Church trend may refuse to enter a church in his own diocese because it is too Catholic for his taste. The dispute about the Prayer-Book, which almost plunged England into a religious revolution a few years ago, was nothing more than a discussion between two branches of the same Church.

At the head of this Church, that is to say, of the

Church of England, are the Archbishops of Canterbury and York, the former of whom is the Primate. Nowadays his influence reaches far beyond the confines of England. He is the Pope of Anglo-Saxon Protestantism and thus one of the sources of England's widespread influence. The higher clergy in England are not restricted to the practice of their actual professional duties. They are admitted to have the right to express themselves with authority upon moral, ethical, and social questions. The tragedy of Edward VIII showed how strong is the power of the Church. It may even intervene in foreign policy, as, for instance, by supporting the League of Nations. Within the country itself its influence is assured by the fact that the Archbishops and some of the Bishops sit in the House of Lords. But the Church has never attempted to take any part in Party politics, still less to found a Party of its own upon a religious basis. Experience has shown that this voluntary restraint has actually strengthened the influence of the Church in the life of the nation, apart from the fact that it means that co-operation between Church and State is practically without friction. The number of full members of the Established Church is reckoned at about two and three-quarter millions, and of the Roman Catholic Church at about two millions. Although Roman Catholicism has greatly strengthened its position in England, it still occupies the place of a tolerated religion, the disciples of which must be on their guard not to wound the susceptibilities of their compatriots, who are, when all is said and done, a Protestant people. Very much more influential are the Free Churches of the Nonconformists, headed by the

Methodist, which numbers a million or more members. Founded upon the teaching of John Wesley, this Church lays the chief emphasis upon personal religious experience and inspired conversion. The Baptists, who believe in adult baptism, form another great religious community with over half a million members, as also do the Congregationalists, in whose eyes the local assembly of the faithful represents the whole Church, with the result that they refuse to submit to any external clerical authority. To name only a few more among many, there are the Presbyterians, the very influential Quakers, and recently Dr. Buchman's Oxford Groups. This multiplicity of sects is the reason why small villages may contain half a dozen Churches and Chapels and Meeting-houses.

The remarkable thing about the whole situation is that the Established Church and the various sects work side by side in perfect accord. In fact, recent years have shown a distinct tendency to rapprochement between the Established Low Church and the Free Churches, both of which communities are coming more and more to be in opposition to the High Anglican Church. While the High Church regards its religion more or less from a purely spiritual, metaphysical aspect, the Low Church and the Nonconformists are at one in their inclination to practical Christianity in the form of social work such as the care of the unemployed and peace propaganda. On this account Low Church influence is growing stronger among the masses, and it is being still further strengthened by means of the wireless. It is the Low Church clergy in particular who make use of the wireless system, which has come to be a very important factor in the religious life of England.

In addition to clerical broadcasters there are also clerical journalists, with Dean Inge at their head. Not that the English clergy discuss the Epistles and Gospels in the daily Press, but they express themselves upon the questions of the day, such as the divorce laws, birth-control, the protection of animals, drink, short skirts, or the use of lipstick. In this way the demand that the clergy should be more in touch with everyday life is fulfilled, even if they thereby may do less work in the pulpit. The fact that the clergy really are more in touch with the people may perhaps atone for the figures recently arrived at by Dr. Matthews, the Dean of St. Paul's, when he calculated that only about twenty per cent. of the inhabitants of England might properly be called Christians.

The English Church would be in a sorry state if this were to mean that the remaining eighty per cent. of the population had turned away altogether from Christianity. But this is certainly not the case in a country like England, in which the working classes in particular have never cared for anti-religious propaganda, but in some form or another—generally Nonconformist—cling firmly to Christianity. Lansbury, the venerable ex-leader of the Labour Party, looks at life far more from a Christian than from a political point of view. He is not a great politician, but perhaps he is the best Christian in the country.

The Church is one of England's two great moral institutions. The other is the Law. And in the course of historical evolution it has happened that they both ultimately meet in the same place—the House of Lords. The highest spiritual Lords as well as the highest Law Lords sit in the Upper House, which thus becomes not merely a political but also a juridical body, being indeed founded upon the royal Courts of Justice of mediæval days. In imperial Germany the administrative officials occupied a much more prominent position than the judges. In England the administrative officials lead a shadow existence, while the judge is surrounded by the pomp of majesty. Possibly there is too much pomp that has to be paid for by the people. Whatever may be the advantages of English judicial administration, it is too dear. It seems curiously out of keeping with modern ideas, moreover, that the Chief Justice of England should be more highly paid than the Prime Minister, as though it were more necessary to prevent his being exposed to the temptations of bribery. The saying that the Englishman's word is his bond must not be taken too literally. Anyone embarking on any sort of legal transaction in England, even if it is only the signing of a lease, will meet with complications and red tape, agents, solicitors, and sealed parchments, such as have long been relegated to oblivion in Germany. As soon as he enters the legal sphere, the otherwise easy-going Englishman becomes bureaucratic and pedantic.

Recently, it is true, England has begun to make some attempt to lessen legal costs by a generous measure of relief for poor persons, just as it has made Eton and Oxford accessible to the poorer classes by means of scholarships. But even so it provides no real remedy for the fact that litigation is a costly luxury. Anyone who loses a case in England is wiser to pay and be done with it. If he lodges an appeal, he may be risking a fortune. Legal costs and lawyers' fees are so high that a case may comparatively easily run up a bill of costs of ten thousand pounds or more. No doubt England's great barristers enjoy earning fifty thousand pounds a year and being raised to the status of national heroes. But this does not further the cause of the ideal "justice for all"—though it may be conceded that the high cost of justice minimizes the danger of immoderate litigation.

Similarly, the way in which cases are publicly tried in England may be looked at from two points of view. The passionate interest taken by the people in its legal administration is admirable. It may be said that popular opinion exercises a kind of supervision over it. The whole country will express its dissatisfaction if a judgment goes against its feelings of what is right, just as a fair and clever judgment is read with the keenest enjoyment. The English bench of judges has its "stars," just as have film and stage, who are known and revered throughout the country. A word from the mouth of such a judge therefore has a moral force that goes far beyond the mere subject of the case, and may make of the judge a teacher of the people. Unfortunately, lesser minds are by this system exposed to the danger of legal vanity, which only too frequently expresses itself in pretentious platitudes.

It is a less pleasing circumstance when England's healthy interest in the judicial administration turns to a morbid enjoyment of crime and immorality. The connection between law and the Press in this case shows the English character in one of its least pleasant lights. As soon as anyone is brought up before a court he is fair game for the lowest type of journalism, which has no interest in justice, but rather in the love of sensation, of the titillation of the nerves, and especially in the circulation of the less responsible newspapers. This type of journalism had gone to such lengths that a law had to be passed to keep at least the reports of divorce scandals within the bounds of decency. The orgy of journalistic indecency to which every famous case led is, however, only decreased and not stopped. What German newspaper would ever dream of dishing up a murder case in a diluted literary form years after the execution of the murderer? Even if the fictional detective story may have something to be said in its favour, the sensational reports of real crimes in the form in which this is done by the English Press is not healthy reading for the public.

To return from crime to judges and the Law. The foundation of English Law is the Common Law, which has grown up piecemeal throughout the centuries. It is utterly opposed to the invariability of Roman Law and has hitherto found no Justinian to codify it. Except where he is bound by particular Acts of Parliament, an English judge delivers judgment according to precedent. At the same time he himself may be creating precedents and turning *jus dicere* into *jus dare*. The responsibility resting on English judges is therefore enormous and explains both the high position occupied by them and the great publicity given to legal pronouncements. The whole nation and not merely a legal code keeps watch to ensure that Law and Justice should remain synonymous. A barrister must spend a long apprenticeship before he reaches the Supreme Court of London, or before he—literally to the accompaniment of drums and trumpets—enters provincial cities as a Judge of the Assize Court. After the completion of his studies and further legal preliminaries, he begins work in a barrister's office. Contrary to German custom, barristers and judges are not two separate professions. In England no one can become a judge who has not first been a barrister. The barrister is quite distinct, however, from the solicitor, who only enjoys very restricted rights of appearing in court, and whose chief occupation consists in the administration of property, drawing up agreements, and other work of a similar nature. Judge and barrister are links in one chain which England values greatly, since it sees a means of consolidation of the sense of justice in this professional corporateness of its legal class. Disputes between judges and barristers occur very seldom indeed.

England's lowest court is that of the Justices of the Peace, the magistrate. To be Justice of the Peace is an honorary post, and only in large towns is such a justice a lawyer and in receipt of a salary. He deals only with the smallest civil law cases, such as disputes about the wages of domestic servants. More important is the significance of this court as the first step in criminal proceedings. The Justice of the Peace must decide whether a delinquency is sufficiently serious to be transferred to a higher court. It is at his discretion to pronounce the fateful words "I commit for trial." The next higher court may be either Quarter Sessions or a Court of Assize. The Quarter Sessions, a criminal court, consist of all the Justices of the Peace in the county, over whom a lawyer, called the Recorder, presides in the towns only. They deal with criminal cases of lesser gravity. The corresponding civil cases up to disputes concerning about a hundred pounds come within the jurisdiction of the fifty-five County Courts of England and Wales that deal with a million cases annually. These courts are presided over by salaried County Court judges.

The higher courts, however, begin only at the next stage—the Assizes, which are both civil and criminal courts. Here is to be found one of the greatest curiosities of English legal administration that is a direct relic of the days when the King travelled about the country to do justice. The County Court judges move about within what is known as a circuit, but the Assizes are truly peripatetic courts. Three times a year the Judges of Assize make solemn entry into various provincial towns, and hear the most serious criminal and civil cases. London alone among English municipalities possesses a permanent higher Court of Justice for civil and criminal cases. The latter is the court known as the Old Bailey.

As in politics, so London is also the country's centre and apex in law. The Supreme Court sits here. It is divided into two parts—the Court of Appeal and the High Court of Justice. The latter is again subdivided into the Chancery Division, the King's Bench, and the Probate, Admiralty, and Divorce Courts in one. The Chancery Court, which was originally a court for the settlement and adjustment of irregularities arising out of the Customary Law, is nowadays occupied with patents, mortgages, trusts, etc., while the King's Bench, at the head of which is the Lord Chief Justice, is the central court for important civil cases. The Assize Judges are chosen from the judges of the King's Bench both for civil and criminal cases. The civil Court of Appeal is called simply the Court of Appeal, while for criminal cases there is the Court of Criminal Appeal. The highest court in the whole country is the House of Lords, which disposes annually of fifty or sixty civil and criminal cases.

Thus legal actions take the following course: for civil there is first the Justice of the Peace, then the County Court, then the Provincial Assizes, then the High Court in London, then the Court of Appeal, and finally the House of Lords. Criminal cases begin with the Justice of the Peace, and go on to Quarter Sessions, Provincial Assizes (in London the Old Bailey), the Court of Criminal Appeal, and the House of Lords. The sequence of courts is something like that in Germany, but it is not really safe to make comparisons, because the differences are too great. Except in the Courts of Appeal, England prefers the one-judge system, makes use of juries in civil cases, divorce proceedings, for example, and has its own system of criminal prosecution. Only in serious cases that concern the public welfare does the Director of Public Prosecutions make his appearance, while as a general rule the duty of prosecution lies with the police or the plaintiff. It is of a piece with the individualism of the Englishman that he should make sparing use of the State's right of punishment and let the goddess of Justice close an eye even under her bandage unless the injured person himself demands redress.

Always supposing that the goddess's eyes are bandaged. And here England, which is justifiably proud of the impartiality of its judges, has nothing with which to reproach itself. That these majestic personages, who are addressed as "My Lord," may sometimes be very harsh is less their fault than that of the law, which sees no reason for mitigating the punishment if the criminal confesses, and which makes no allowance for the *crime passionel*. An eye for an eye, a tooth for a tooth, says the law of to-day with the Old Testament severity that England learnt in the school of Calvinism. Hence it is not surprising to find that corporal punishment has survived in English Law, as in English schools. During the year 1935 thirty criminals found guilty of assault and sexual offences were given the "cat," the notorious nine-tailed whip. There were, however, in addition, two hundred and eleven boys between the ages of eight and fourteen who were condemned by magistrates to be birched. While the English treat their animals with kindness that verges on sentimentality, and as a consequence condemn those who are found guilty of cruelty to animals to the most severe punishments, they treat their erring fellow-man with great severity. England believes in the deterrent effects of punishment, and it must be admitted that its recent experience with the intensification of the punishment for blackmail has proved it to be right. In post-War years blackmail threatened to become a fashionable crime from which no one was safe, until the law intervened with merciless severity and with undeniable success. A less serious offence, and one peculiar to England, is bigamy. Not only the proverbial sailor has a wife in every port, but the simple, matter-of-fact Englishman is apt to act in the same way. The tendency to rash marriage is common to all classes of the population.

As in other countries, the right of pardon is the prerogative of the Crown, which makes use of it at the recommendation of the Home Secretary. A condemned person is, however, seldom pardoned and usually only when the court itself recommends mercy. Anyone who commits murder in England must reckon with the noose, all the more so since he is, as it were, trapped by living on an island where only harbours and not frontiers have to be watched. Furthermore, after a crime has been committed, a man-hunt begins in which the whole population takes part, and especially the Press. For reasons into which it is not necessary to enter here, the Press puts itself freely at the disposal of the police in order to help catch the criminal. Photographs, letters, and every imaginable clue are published in the Press, and popular imagination is stimulated to such a degree by the dramatic presentation of the crime that even school-children keep a watch for the outlaw. A highly-developed science of criminology and a model police force do the rest.

In a country which contains as many reformers as England, it is natural that its system of justice should by some people be regarded as mediæval. Recently a highly sensational agitation was started for the abolition of the death penalty, although there is little likelihood of its being done away with in the near future. It seems immensely more important in the public opinion that the English divorce laws should be reformed, as is being attempted now,[1] the old law having led to abuses which mock every feeling of justice. In practice the English law allows divorce only for adultery. Hence people who wish to be divorced are obliged to commit adultery, or at all events to simulate it. If the latter method is decided upon, legal firms of doubtful standing will provide a lady, a room in an hotel, and possibly even a detective as witness. The "injured wife" may then carry through the divorce proceedings upon grounds thus provided, with the hotel bill, which is sent her by the husband himself, to prove her claim. Thus she is able to divorce her husband, instead of being divorced, and so honour is satisfied, even though the real fault may lie with the wife. Hence an Englishwoman does not say "I have been divorced," but "I divorced my husband" —the husband who from motives of chivalry agreed to go through with the unpleasant farce. The person who is in the greatest danger in English divorce cases is the third member of the triangle—the co-respondent. The courts may condemn him to pay a considerable fine to the injured party. The same habit of making good purely moral damage by monetary satisfaction is seen again in the "breach-of-promise" case which a girl may bring against her lover. It must be said, however, in fairness to Englishwomen, that these cases are brought very seldom nowadays. On the other hand, divorce proceedings have multiplied greatly, and this fact is one of the gravest sources of disquiet to the Church of England. It serves to explain its opposition to the

[1] Since this was written the Bill has been passed by Parliament.

marriage of Edward VIII with Mrs. Simpson, who had been twice divorced, which cost the King his crown.

A final peculiarity of English Law is the enormously high damages that are given for libel. Historically they are accounted for by the legal abolition of duelling, which was so thorough that duels are completely unknown in England now. As a result it was found necessary to provide legal protection for personal honour. The law of libel is all the more severe because proof of the truth of a statement does not save the culprit from punishment. Printed libels, especially, are a major crime in the eyes of the individualistic Englishman. Hence newspaper and other publishers at times have their publications looked at by lawyers specially appointed by them for the work to make sure that they contain nothing libellous, neglect of which might cost them a fortune. In mentioning the lack of restraint in the reports of the English Press, it should be added that they are kept within bounds to some extent by the law of libel.

England's State structure is woven firmly but loosely; its Law is elastic and yet rigid. Both State and Law are bound to the past by hundreds of links, and yet both are up to date. Hard as England finds it to separate itself from its history, it is not reactionary. Nor is its Church, where many good brains are working to bring the eternal verities into harmony with the demands of the present day. The individual Englishman is easy-going, but his great institutions are strong and full of majesty. It is because England has for centuries refused to be ruled by an autocrat that it reveres the Law, both human and divine. This law-abiding temperament, which is found throughout the nation and which Rome left as a great heritage to conquered Britain, is the counterpoise to English individualism. Independent as the individual Englishman may be, he recognizes the higher powers that are set in authority over him.

CHAPTER VIII

ENGLISH CIVILIZATION

BRITONS and Romans, Celts and Anglo-Saxons, Danes and Normans—these were the ancestors of the modern Englishman. His history and his racial origins alike cause the Englishman to feel himself the heir to many civilizations. Greece and Rome contributed their share to his physical and mental education. His debt to France is large for much of his language and many of his habits of life. Germany gave him religious and scientific ideas. Holland powerfully influenced English architecture. The Englishman, nevertheless, looks upon himself as Germanic or, as he himself prefers to express it, Teutonic by blood and temperament. An exception to this general rule is, however, to be found in the Celtic element in the English population, whose proudest boast even to-day is that they are Celts. The Celts are a foreign substance in the political and racial composition of the English nation. They regard themselves as such and are so regarded by the remainder of the population. An Englishman who feels himself at home in Hamburg feels himself to be a foreigner in Wales and still more so in Ireland. The gulf which separates the Englishman from the Celt is indeed far deeper and broader than that which divides the harsh and forbidding northern Englishman from his friendlier and more approachable southern compatriot.

It is an historical fact of extraordinary interest that the English, who have conferred their civilization upon the remotest peoples in the world, have wholly failed to win acceptance for it from the Celts living at their doors. The political genius that created a world empire deserted them in their governance of Ireland. Wales has certainly been incorporated into the English kingdom. Nevertheless, England has been unable to induce the Welsh to accept its civilization. Its failure is all the more remarkable since no religious barrier intervenes, as in Ireland, between the two races. The Welsh are Methodists; the Irish Roman Catholics. The Methodism of John Wesley is the negation of Roman Catholicism in its substitution of an inner and individual spiritual life for the rule of an organized and authoritarian Church. The mysticism that is so alien to the severely practical English mind finds its natural home in that of the Celt, where, as is so often the case, it unites with a keen and wholly un-English love of intellectual pursuits and pastimes. The Celt is impulsive and emotional. He is reproached by the English for his instability and untrustworthiness. It is for this reason that the greatest of living Celts, David Lloyd George, has failed to gain the confidence of the English people. Although he led them to victory in the World War, Lloyd George has never ceased in their eyes to be the "Welsh wizard"; and when there was no longer any necessity for him to wave his magic wand Lloyd George returned to being the stranger in their midst.

It is undoubtedly true that the Celtic temperament is not free from a strain of cruelty that found a terrible outlet in the Irish Civil War. If the Englishman is the master of his emotions, the Celt is only too frequently the slave of his passions. The Englishman has organized his forces for practical ends. The Celt, on the other hand, finds in art the outlet for his romantic yearnings and creative impulses. England owes the immortal Arthurian legends to the Celtic love of imagery and romance; and a Celt—the Irishman George Bernard Shaw—is the embodiment of the malicious, critical, and often destructive intellect and wit of his race. It is, nevertheless, in the world of music that the contrast between Celts and English reveals itself most clearly. If by "music" is understood folk-music, the Celts are to be numbered among the most musical of peoples. Every evening the mountain valleys of Wales echo to the sound of tragic strains sung by choirs. The Welsh might compete successfully with the Russians for the title of the world's greatest choral singers. It is therefore astonishing that so musical a people should have hitherto failed to produce a single great composer.

The reason for this failure is possibly to be found in a gradual drying-up of the ancient Celtic springs of fancy. Or, perhaps, the racial spirit has become so weakened that it lacks the stamina necessary for the accomplishment of great achievements. Or is it that the many defeats sustained by the Celts in the course of their tragic history have robbed them of the self-confidence that is the Englishman's deepest source of strength? An atmosphere of melancholy surrounds the Celts, whose lives seem to be passed now on one, now on the other side of the border that divides the real from the unreal. It was their inability to be wholly of this world that enabled the more worldly English to deprive the Celts of their earthly possessions. Now that Ireland is no longer of the same importance in English eyes the Irish are free to govern themselves. It was the Celt Lloyd George who gave his Celtic brothers across the Irish Sea this great opportunity of realizing their dreams. Time alone will show whether the attempt is to be crowned with success. The pages of Celtic history are filled with the record of promising beginnings that ended in failure.

However much the English may have taken from the Celts by force, the Celts themselves have voluntarily given the English at least as much again. The English character cannot be understood aright if the Celtic strain in it is forgotten. It is English literature above all else that has been enriched by the Celts with their love of metaphysics and their passionate Christianity no less than with their profound feeling for Nature. Undoubtedly much that derives from Celtic influences is unintelligible to an English reader. In Wales, for example, where Bardic customs still survive, Welsh is spoken and written: a language that cannot be even properly pronounced by anyone who is not a Celt. The propagation and study of Irish in post-War Ireland is not unnaturally intended to serve political ends. A similar movement in the Highlands and in the islands off the west coast of Scotland is free from any political tendency. Scotland, like Wales, has long since reconciled itself to being an integral part of the United Kingdom, within which it is only concerned to preserve its distinctive racial character. Geographical propinquity has proved stronger than political particularism. England therefore places no obstacle in the way of Scotland's realizing this aim.

England has assimilated the civilizations of other countries. Moreover, it has incorporated into its State system those portions of the British Isles that naturally form a political whole, even though they are inhabited by different races. England is the sum total of these parts. The existence of the individual parts nevertheless explains the sharp contrasts and conflicts that characterize English political and intellectual life. Charles Dickens and Oscar Wilde, Lloyd George and Austen Chamberlain, James Joyce and Thomas Hardy—these men are not only individual personalities but also representatives of widely different worlds. Nevertheless—taken together—they represent England as a whole. It is therefore possible to find a common denominator for English intellectual and civilizatory achievements if these differences are borne in mind. We can begin by considering the most general expression of culturetaste. It is at once possible to distinguish an artistic style that is wholly foreign to English taste—baroque. No style is more alien to English taste than the baroque, with its large and often meaningless gestures, its florid and frequently poor materials. Baroque exaggerates: the Englishman understates. Baroque dramatizes; the Englishman is un-theatrical in all things. The style of the Renaissance is less foreign to English taste. Indeed, England owes to the Renaissance not only its greatest poets but also many of its most beautiful buildings. England underwent a great revolution in taste in 1640 and the succeeding years. These were the years in which the brilliant man of the Renaissance was superseded by the Puritan with his Christian and classical traditions, who ever since has been the standard-bearer of English civilization.

Now that England is liberating itself from the ugliness and want of taste of the Victorian Age the eighteenth century is once more coming into the foreground. Good materials, restraint in the use of ornamentation, and harmonious proportions are to-day England's ideal of beauty. Modern England finds the embodiment of this ideal in the houses built during the Hanoverian period. These so-called "Georgian" houses are square-shaped, built of brick, with the simplest lines. Neither towers nor gables nor even window-shutters disturb the simplicity of buildings whose charm consists in their proportions and the harmonious arrangement of doors and windows. The interior corresponds to the exterior. One encounters here one of the outstanding expressions of English good taste—interior decoration and furnishings.

For centuries England has been a wealthy land. For this reason its finest furniture, unlike that of France and Italy, has not been sold to foreigners. These overlooked the perfection achieved by English furniture-makers and spent their money lavishly on far less admirable rococo furniture. Gilt arabesques were valued more highly than the superbly dignified furniture that is for ever associated with the names of Chippendale, Sheraton, Adam, and Nash. An English connoisseur to-day has no higher ambition than to possess their works. In the history of English furniture the works of these great artists take the place occupied in other countries by the Empire and Biedermeier styles.

Biedermeier furniture is used in England only for the rooms of young girls. Eighteenth-century furniture, on the other hand, is accorded pride of place in dining-rooms, libraries, and drawing-rooms. The aim of every English collector is to acquire eighteenth-century furniture and silver, and the experience he gains in the course of his searches soon makes of him an expert. The Englishman, whose bookshelves are filled with volumes on travel and sport, is a critical connoisseur when it becomes a question of buying a Chippendale chair or a George III tea-caddy. Far more than in Germany, education in England is an education in good taste. By this means also one can easily differentiate between the various classes. His house, and especially its furnishings, is the outward expression of an Englishman's utilitarian good taste. For this reason a beautiful English room is among the most beautiful to be found in Europe. And all the more so because it satisfies the needs of modern life better than the classically furnished French or Italian room. Unlike French and Italian rooms, the English room is furnished not merely for show but also for comfort. Hence the open fireplaces and the candles on the dining-tables. Post-War England recognized the good effect of fine silver set out on perfect wood and gave up using tablecloths on its dining-tables.

If the eighteenth century has not wholly banished the more ornate Jacobean style of the preceding century, it has certainly superseded it in the public taste. The beams and cross-beams of the Tudor period are, nevertheless, so popular that high prices are paid for Tudor houses. Imitations of the Tudor style are in doubtful taste. The modern architect seeks above all else to model himself upon the eighteenth century, whose simplicity he strives to regain. Modern English architecture seeks simplicity, in contrast to that of the nineteenth century, that turned English streets into forests of pillars. An effect that is all the more monotonous because the architect in England thinks in terms of streets rather than houses. When the streets are as beautiful as those built by Nash in Bath, the mass effect is all the more powerful. But an ugly and ill-designed house loses nothing of its ugliness if it is reproduced a hundredfold in the Victorian districts of London. It is only in recent years that fresh inspiration has come to English architects. Many modern private houses in Hampstead or the new Battersea Power Station have no more reason for fearing foreign competition than have certain of London's skyscrapers or the blocks of flats built of brick and faced with white stone. For London is being rebuilt. Old aristocratic houses are being pulled down to make room for the characterless buildings of a capitalist society which reveal very clearly to the passer-by that they are the property not of an individual but of a company. Everything in these buildings is intended to serve utilitarian purposes to such an extent that at times an inhabitant of these Americanized structures feels that he is living in a factory. The effect of uniformity and coldness is still more painful in the blocks of flats that sprang up in post-War years like mushrooms out of the ground. In those days England broke with its age-long tradition of the individual home simply because servants were unobtainable for the housework. It is nevertheless significant that the return of economic prosperity has resulted in an increased demand for private houses. An Englishman sets great store by the undivided possession of his own doorstep.

The dislike of ornamentation revealed by the English in their domestic architecture also extends to their living-rooms. Here the revolution in taste can again be descried that has swept over the country since the Victorians plastered their walls with pictures in a manner only to be found nowadays in the homes of the suburban middle classes. The Englishman of taste is content to possess few but really good pictures and etchings. It is the same in the case of a man with intellectual interests. Only he will accord a space on his walls to examples of modern art that are still excluded from the stately homes of England, where the opinion is still held that a painting is a work of art and not the pictorial expression of an intellectual upheaval. The old furniture that gives its distinctive atmosphere to these houses also needs the harmonious counterparts. The place of honour for a picture in an English house is on the wall over the fireplace. It is there that the outstanding picture in the house is to be found. It will be an example of the Italian, Dutch, or English Schools if the owner is conservative in his tastes. If he is interested in modern art, it is likely to be a modern French painting. Anyone who is unaware of the wealth of England can calculate it from the pictures on the walls of its homes. There he will realize the vastness and richness of its private art collections. Pictures that on the Continent would long ago have found their way into public art galleries still adorn English dining- and drawing-rooms. If taken in conjunction with the American, the English demand for pictures explains the fantastic prices that are paid for works by Gainsborough, Romney, or Reynolds. No matter how greatly an Englishman may admire the works of foreign artists, the first place in his affections is occupied by those of his own countrymen. Here the eighteenth century again takes precedence over all others; especially for portraits. Although England has produced great landscape painters, and, above all, Constable, it is the portrait that has always been the outstanding example of English painting : for portraiture affords the English artist an opportunity of displaying his psychological insight and his gifts of characterization. The fame of Sir John Lavery and of the most gifted of contemporary English painters, Augustus John, is founded upon their portraits. Landscape painting, on the other hand, has been left to the painters in water-colour, whose brilliant technique must be numbered among England's unique artistic achievements. Nobody who visits the Exhibition of the Royal Academy in London should fail to inspect the rooms containing the water-colour paintings. These rooms are not seldom more pleasing in their general effect than those devoted to oil-paintings.

A love of painting in water-colours is inborn in every Englishman. Even when he is not an artist by profession the Englishman amuses himself by painting in water-colours. The number of gifted amateur painters in England is extraordinarily high. And by "amateurs" in this connection is meant really talented painters and not merely schoolgirls playing at painting. The leisure hours that the German devotes to the pianoforte are occupied by the Englishman—no matter whether he be a student, a City man, or even an M.P. spending a week-end in the country—in painting. If Winston Churchill, for example, is not engaged in criticizing the Government or writing a book or building a brick wall, he is to be found busied with brush and canvas. Sir William Eden, the father of Mr. Anthony Eden, was the most gifted amateur painter of his day, who would have become a great artist if fox-hunting had not taken up so much of his time. Moreover, it is significant that neither Eden nor Churchill are exceptions, but instead merely two examples of the typically English habit of having, in addition to a profession, a hobby whose pursuit alleviates the monotony of daily life.

The visual arts of England find expression in architecture, painting, and the applied arts. Among these latter the manufacture of porcelain must not be forgotten, indissolubly connected as it is with the names Wedgwood, Worcester, Chelsea, and Crown Derby. But England has never produced a sculptor of genius. Its greatest sculptor for many generations—Jacob Epstein—is a Jew born in New York. From a creative standpoint English sculpture is poorer in achievement than English music. England, indeed, was once a home of music. In the days of the Tudors and the Stuarts England possessed music of its own composition. But the succeeding age of Puritanism destroyed England's musical creativeness. All that remained to a people who had formerly played and sung was the craving for music: a craving that came in the course of centuries to resemble that of the Germans for politics. While Germany envied England her statesmen, England's eyes were fixed upon the great German composers who gave her the music that she was unable to compose for herself. Light music alone survived and flourished in England. Now and again it produced masterpieces like "The Beggar's Opera" and "The Mikado." But the great oratorios and orchestral works for which England longed above all else came to her from Germany. It is only in recent years that serious music has experienced a revival in England as a consequence of the work of composers such as Elgar, Vaughan Williams, and William Walton. Although England claims Delius as her son, he, like Handel, was the child of German parents. Even as there are Germans who cannot believe that Shakespeare was not a German, so there are English-men who regard Handel as their compatriot. He did indeed give deep and sincere expression to the musical emotions of the country of his choice.

For centuries lively popular songs and serious classical and Church music have made up England's musical diet. On the other hand, opera has been long in coming into its own. The English dislike of baroque has already been commented upon. It was because England believed opera to be a baroque form of music that it found it as alien to its taste as the great Jesuit churches of Southern Germany. Even to-day, when the pioneer efforts of English conductors and wealthy music-lovers have succeeded in making a home for opera, and above all for Wagner's operas, in England, the opera still continues to be looked upon by the masses of the people as a foreign importation. In their eyes opera was something brought from abroad to Covent Garden, where it was played by foreign artists. In this, as in other things, appetite grew with the eating. It soon ceased to suffice that great European singers and conductors were invited to London every spring. If England could not itself produce operatic composers to rank with the great foreign composers, it wished at least to produce foreign operas by the aid of native talent. In Sadler's Wells London acquired its own opera-house, in which seats are available, as compared with Covent Garden, at moderate prices. One of the greatest Mæcenases of his generation, Mr. Christie, created about the same time an English Bayreuth for Mozart at his lovely country home at Glyndebourne in Sussex that need not fear comparison with either Salzburg or Bayreuth itself. As so often before in England, private enterprise and generosity stepped in to fill the gap which the State left vacant. Unlike Germany, which looks upon its opera-houses and theatres as great centres for popular education, England has always refused to subsidize the drama or music. It is therefore all the more remarkable and praiseworthy that opera-lovers in England, with the famous conductor Sir Thomas Beecham at their head, should have been able to achieve so much by their own unaided resources. Thanks to their efforts opera has come into its own in England to-day, even though it has not yet been possible to create a national opera: an aim that seems exceptionally difficult of accomplishment without the presence of great English composers.

It is only since the World War that London has become a permanent and first-class home of opera: a fact that witnesses of itself to the immense progress made by England in recent years in musical matters. This is also shown with equal clarity in the concert world. Although London has always been famous for its concerts, it is to-day pre-eminent in the world.

There is not a living conductor who would not regard it as an honour to be invited to London, where he finds first-rate orchestras, unrivalled choirs, and audiences and musical critics who are not satisfied with any but the best performances. Whoever—musically speaking—passes muster in London need fear no criticism anywhere else; whoever makes a name for himself in London is immediately a world-wide celebrity. Although musical circles in London are fundamentally conservative in taste, they do not refuse a hearing for the most modern compositions. Alongside the names of the great planets of the London concert world—Beethoven, Mozart, Handel, and Bach—there appear on the programmes those of Debussy, Strauss, Ravel, Sibelius, and the Russian composers. These latter are responsible for the fact that post-War London has also become a great centre of ballet where three or even four troupes can perform simultaneously in different theatres to crowded houses.

It is therefore a mistake to call the artistic life of England old-fashioned or conventional. Anyone who does so is himself conventional. Indeed, it is as if French literature were to be judged solely by the works of the French Academicians. England to-day is filled with rebellious and self-willed spirits intent upon discovering new artistic paths. No matter how bound by tradition England may be, it never permits itself to be reduced to inertia by its past. The best English musicians, like the latest generation of painters represented in the London Group, are the children of their age. Futurist and Dadaist exhibitions are held in London that are visited by an interested—if critical—public. Guardians of

Victorian standards of artistic taste do, indeed, pour tar upon Epstein's statues, shut their ears to modern music, and scream for the Censor if they happen upon a psychological novel. Over against them stands a generation resolved to go forward and ready to risk any experiment that promises to lead them to fresh discoveries.

Notwithstanding the notable achievements of English painters and architects, it is in the world of literature that to-day as formerly England's greatest artistic triumphs are won. Ever since Chaucer gave literary form to the English language each passing century has produced poets and writers of genius. When all else failed literature remained a living force and an unquenchable source of national inspiration. In literature England's national spirit, as Germany's in music, found its fullest expression. Even if every age was not an Augustan, the great procession of English writers continued uninterruptedly, and each succeeding generation made its own contribution to the national literature after its own fashion.

A great and wonderfully harmonious work of art was thus gradually achieved that will bear witness to England long after its world empire has crumbled into dust. England has raised an imperishable monument in its literature to its own greatness.

It seems necessary at this point to say something about the English language. English is a mixed language, not only because it is a compound of German and Latin words but also because two different classes in society simultaneously adopted it as their medium of expression. After the Norman Conquest French and Latin were the languages of the educated laity and clergy, and the native language sank very nearly to the level of a peasant dialect. The peasants in the villages used a language among themselves that was simple and easy to understand rather than distinguished by logical processes of thought or rhetorical beauty. This peasant English spread like wild flowers that spontaneously produce thousands of varieties. Centuries passed, until one day this peasant dialect was raised from its low estate and beautified by the language of the educated classes. From this strange marriage was born the English language, the nature of which can only be understood if its parentage is called to mind. English is as uninflected as the speech of common folk and its syntax is as simple. Why make use of involved sentences when it suffices to link up one sentence with another? Why use long words merely to talk to a neighbour? Why puzzle one's brains with a logical sequence in writing? Without destroying the popular character of the language Court circles gave to it the necessary polish and courtliness, the fine shades of meaning, and many expressions unknown to the common people. The mingling of these two elements made the English language with which Shakespeare wrote the greatest of all poetry two centuries after Chaucer's death.

The years of intellectual effervescence were followed by the age of Puritanism, which left its mark of moderation and coldness upon the language. At the same time the theatre fell into disfavour, and the novel and lyrical poetry took its place in popular esteem. Shakespeare and the great epic poet Milton were isolated phenomena. On the other hand, the long chain of English novelists has never been broken from Defoe, Swift,

Fielding, Sterne, Jane Austen, Dickens, Thackeray, and the Brontës to Thomas Hardy, Conrad, George Moore, and present-day writers. Each successive generation made its individual contribution to an English prose style of which the mastery has become so general that a newspaper like *The Times* may justly boast that very fine English prose is to be found in its leading articles. Here it is possible to watch the Englishman playing upon his literary instrument and to distinguish the different notes. English prose must flow quietly and steadily without losing its way in shallows or sudden and unexpected rapids. There must be neither high nor low tones, nor an involved construction that obscures the meaning. Lengthy periods are merely a succession of short sentences loosely joined to each other. If a writer cannot bind his sentences together artistically he may unconcernedly make use of short—even very short—sentences after the fashion of many of the best contemporary writers. In similar fashion short words are nowadays preferred to long, simple to obscure, English to foreign: for nothing is looked upon as in worse taste than a pompous, bombastic, or rhetorical style. Anyone guilty of using such a style commits the most heinous offence against the great traditions of the English language. For English should be simple and clear, or at any rate give the appearance of simplicity and clearness, after the manner of the Englishman himself, who assumes a look of innocence when he wishes to deceive. Anyone who hears an Englishman declare that he is a plain and ordinary man had better be on his guard. Such language is only employed by a man seeking to entrap his fellow.

Similarly, the English language both spoken and written is less naïve than it would appear. This fact does not prevent the language from serving as a superb means of expression when simplicity and sincerity are genuinely sought after. English can be as crystalline and translucent as a diamond. At the same time it is also rich in hidden meanings, suggestion, and in all that enables the hearer or reader to perceive the meaning that lies between the lines. A witty Englishman observed once that it was difficult to speak the truth in French or to lie in German, whilst English was equally suitable for either lying or telling the truth. For this reason alone—he added—English was predestined to be a universal language. The saying contains a truth that also serves to reveal the English character. The art displayed by the Englishman in avoiding committing himself, except when absolutely necessary, finds expression in a language that can be turned as by the wave of a magic wand into a veil behind which its user can escape from his would-be captors. Nevertheless, English lacks nothing in distinctness. It is merely that the language is extraordinarily supple and capable of serving every type of speaker in every kind of emergency. English can equal the finest French for delicacy; it can sound affected on the lips of suburban women; and in ports and harbours it can change into the foulest language in the world. Nothing can sound more horrible than two common women brawling in English. Neither French nor Italian sink to such depths. How sweet and melodious, on the other hand, the same language sounds on the lips of the poet! How lightly and easily the sentences flow on a page of good English prose!

How readily the words suit themselves to the dry humour of the land! And, above all, how practical is language that enables a writer of a letter to begin with "Dear Sir" and to end with "Yours sincerely" no matter who may be his correspondent! Every commercial apprentice can write a letter that is to be understood by a foreigner with only a slight knowledge of the language. If one ignores the extremely difficult spelling, English must be accounted among the most easily learnt languages; more especially if it is only a question of using it superficially.

England has also every reason to be proud of the style of its scientific writings. It is a pleasure to read learned English books, whose authors resolutely refuse to employ a scientific jargon. Difficulties only begin when it becomes necessary to find words to express abstract concepts, because English is poor in such words. One of the limitations is here touched upon of a language that is primarily intended to serve practical ends and that works best when it is necessary to give expression to facts. It is for this reason that works of history and biography have always been among the gems of English literature.

The greatest civilizing weapon in England's hands is its language. It was indeed a unique stroke of luck for England that such a language was ready to its hand when English soldiers set out on the conquest of the world and English merchants began trading with foreign peoples. Even as England robbed the French of one colony after the other, so the English language gradually superseded the French, that had long prided itself on being universal and the language of diplomacy. Where-ever the English came, their language revealed itself as capable of use—though often in a debased form. Germans themselves are not free from such mistakes, inasmuch as in their desire to speak good English they often try to be more English than the Englishman himself. No educated Englishman ever makes use of the guttural sounds that are emitted by so many Germans in speaking English, any more than an educated German utters the shish-like "ch" that arouses the Englishman's sense of humour. A German learning English would therefore do well to let himself be warned against exaggerations. Although it is possible that among common people or in America and the Colonies English is spoken as if a hot potato were held in the mouth, this is not the speech of the cultured Englishman. If the German desires to imitate his manner of speech, let him do it unaffectedly and to the best of his natural ability: the time and trouble thus saved may be well employed in seeking to acquire the intonation the absence of which enables the Englishman to recognize the foreigner even in a German speaking grammatical English. In comparison with German the English language lacks emphasis. Hence the English complain that Germans "bark" rather than talk. English, on the contrary, must sound "casual"; that is to say, spoken lightly and as if the speaker was not specially interested in what he was saying. This light and casual manner of speech is consonant with the general behaviour of an Englishman, and is so natural to him that it is almost impossible of imitation by a foreigner. For the same reason English as spoken by foreigners sounds noisy in English ears. Nevertheless, the Englishman is not annoyed by this, because he is so little endowed with the gift of languages that he admires even the poorest linguistic efforts of a foreigner. It must, however, be said at once that those Englishmen who possess a talent for languages are great linguists, just as a musical Englishman is musical indeed. In this, as in other spheres, the contrasts are sharper in England than in Germany.

Apart from Shakespeare, the novel and the lyric are England's chief forms of literary expression. Throughout the years when the theatre was under the ban of a moral censorship lyric poetry, which had produced its most lovely flowers during the reign of Queen Elizabeth, continued to flourish. England's love of form, its pleasure in melodious language, its love of nature, and its sentimentality constantly received fresh inspiration in its poetry. Nevertheless, England has never produced a lyrical genius comparable to Goethe. Moreover, premature death robbed English literature of two of its greatest poets, Shelley and Keats. The metaphysical nature poetry of Wordsworth cannot compensate for this loss, although his poetry contributed greatly to deepen and strengthen the love of nature inborn in his compatriots. At the same time the English poet remained exposed to the danger of identifying Nature with a garden and of adorning his verses with a herbaceous border. It is therefore easy to understand why a rebellious or penetrating intellect like Swinburne's or D. H. Lawrence's produces the effect of a strong and invigorating wind blowing across the fields of English poetry. Nevertheless, these ardent spirits, like Byron and Shelley before them, were ostracized by their countrymen. The same England that has accorded an asylum to every political revolutionary has shown itself hardhearted towards its poets. The lives of the English poets are an epic in themselves, from which may be learnt all that a great genius can suffer in the way of loneliness and want of recognition. Only when the grave has closed over him is recognition given to his achievement. At the same time, poetry is popular in a country which still places a Poet Laureate at the head of its poets. Many more Englishmen than might appear upon the surface are poets by nature and lovers of poetry, even though they do not compose it themselves. In college rooms at Oxford and Cambridge there are to be found not only sporting and film journals but also—to name only a few among England's contemporary poets—the poems of Housman, Eliot, Blunden, and Squire.

A novelist naturally finds a far wider circle of readers. Moreover, this is especially true when he writes in a style that can be easily understood by millions of readers all over the world. No matter how important English poetry may be, the English novel exercises a deeper and more widespread influence. It is the English novel—Shakespeare being once again excepted—that constitutes England's greatest contribution to the literature of the world. Although every variety of fiction is to be found, the "Entwicklungsroman" is the Cinderella of this great family. The basic theme of the novelists of a nation averse to self-analysis is the relationship between man and man in all its innumerable aspects rather than introspective monologue or man in his relationship to God. The English novel thus becomes a picture of contemporary life and its author the portrayer of the social conditions of his time among the proletarian, peasant, aristocratic, or middle classes. If England possesses few novels of the kind of the "Lehr- und Wanderjahre" or "Grüner Heinrich," it can pride itself upon a great wealth of first-rate novels of social life. Nor is this astonishing in a country whose inhabitants possess such marked social instincts and such a capacity for forming social groups within the nation. Every social, indeed every professional, group develops by means of strongly marked idiosyncrasies and conventions into an entity that can easily be distinguished from any other entity. The interest in sociology and the matchless power of observation that are common to all Englishmen find a welcome field of activity in the study of the characteristics of these different groups. Nothing escapes the keen eyes of the English novelist, whose vision is all the clearer because he never loses his inborn detachment. Despite the acute psychological insight revealed in the English novel, it must not be compared with psychological and psychopathological Scandinavian and Russian novels. The Englishman dislikes chaotic or morbid probings and problems that do not admit of a solution. (In this respect D. H. Lawrence is only the exception that proves the rule.) The common man seems to him to be sufficiently interesting if only he is portrayed in a lifelike and intelligible manner. Thomas Hardy, Conrad, Francis Brett Young, Hugh Walpole, Priestley, Galsworthy, Arnold Bennett, and H. G. Wells have never created characters of the colossal proportions of the Raskolnikoffs or Goesta Berling. But they have filled their novels with brilliantly contrasted types of ordinary humanity. The instant the English novelist takes up his pen he reveals himself as a master of the novelist's technique that has become as fully developed in the course of its long history as the parliamentary procedure of Westminster. The traditional technique has, however, ceased to satisfy at least one gifted novelist in the person of Aldous Huxley, who has therefore, as in his latest novel "Eyeless in Gaza," experimented in a new form or else written his stories in the form of essays. In adapting the essay to the purpose of the novelist Huxley has invaded one of the most magnificent provinces of English literature. From time immemorial the essay has been held in high esteem in England among a people who delight to subject social conditions to penetrating analysis and criticism and to illuminate every corner of life by the powerful light of reason. Even to-day Voltaire continues to influence English intellectual life, just as later French prose has left its mark upon English literature. Among modern French writers Anatole France and Proust are known to a wide circle of English readers.

In very recent days America has made its appearance above the English literary horizon. For English readers believe that across the Atlantic the novel is assuming new forms. Literary circles in the older country are gazing in astonishment and even stupefaction at the vast raw material which stands ready to the hands of young American writers. In comparison England's stores of raw material are showing signs of exhaustion, and if it were not that new writers of genius are constantly making their appearance, as recently Charles Morgan, the English novel would suffer from a monotonous uniformity. While the American novelist is able to make use of an inexhaustible wealth of material, the English writer is forced to husband his resources and to make up for his want of fresh inspiration by an increasingly perfect technique. In the case of D. H. Lawrence, for example, the thirst for deep and invigorating sources of inspiration was incapable of being quenched by those at his disposal. Is there not also a literary flavour about Chesterton's Catholicism that is foreign to sincere faith? Notwithstanding the enormous output, English literature does not suffer from exuberance. For it is the product of a nation that has attained maturity, and that without despising the new is still able to pursue old paths, because it possesses the strength that enables it to go forward along them. To-day, as yesterday, the English novelist is a superb story-teller endowed with the gift of making an imaginary or real happening take place before his reader's eyes. How magnificently Kipling, who died recently, could tell a story! Similarly, the English literary humorist shows no signs of failing powers. Jerome K. Jerome's "Three Men in a Boat" will live on long after his death, and Max Beerbohm's work, unlike Max Beerbohm himself, is ageless. A journalist is even to be found among the most popular humorists of the day. The column that appears in the *Daily Express* under the pseudonym of "Beachcomber" is, to some readers, worth more than the whole of the rest of the paper. Beside the humorist stands the satirist, who finds an unfailing source of inspiration in the rich, newly rich, and pleasure-seeking society of London or the narrow-minded and conventional middle classes. All the vanities, cynicism, and vices of the present day are reproduced in contemporary novels. No matter what its artistic value may be, the novel is an inexhaustible source for the future historian of society and manners—and an exceedingly amusing one into the bargain. For authors of this type of novel, like the brothers Evelyn and Alec Waugh, are alive to the impatience of the modern reader avid of excitement and humour. It is only an outstandingly great writer, like George Moore, whose "Brook Kerith" is numbered among the classics of English literature, or one of the originality of James Joyce, who can permit himself to write long novels after the fashion of the older English novelists. The less gifted among modern writers must suit the pace of stories to the desire for swift movement of a cinema-going public. This is especially true of writers of purely imaginary stories—so-called "fiction."

As elsewhere, so also in England these writers have to contend to-day with the competition of writers of works in which real events or persons are described under the guise of fiction. Lytton Strachey was the pioneer in this field of literature, whose followers— Robert Graves with his "Claudius" novels may be mentioned here—have been numerous. A parallel to this type of pseudo-historical novel is formed by the biography proper—a branch of literature that has been developed with the utmost care in England. No country in the world reveals itself more grateful for political services than does England, which does not leave its great men to moulder in their graves unknown to posterity but instead raises memorials to them in the form of biographies. The former editor of *The Times*, Buckle, wrote the standard biography of Disraeli; the editor of the *Observer*, Garvin, that of Joseph Chamberlain; whilst the present Secretary of State for War,

Duff Cooper, has followed up his life of Talleyrand by a biography of Field-Marshal Haig. Winston Churchill delved into the archives of his family and enriched English literature with a brilliant portrait of his great ancestor, the Duke of Marlborough. Out of his own experiences Churchill wrote his famous account of the World War, whilst Lloyd George embodied his war memories in a monumental work extending to six volumes, an achievement that freed him from the reproach of being an amateur of letters. If this reproach was unmerited in Lloyd George's case, it was still more so in that of Winston Churchill, whose bitterest political opponents cannot deny him his literary laurels. It speaks volumes for the high standard of English culture that it is possible for those who only pursue it as a hobby to achieve a great name in literature. As in all other departments of English life, so also in literature there is no reproach attached to the designation of amateur. On the contrary, much that is greatest in English life has been the work of amateurs. An outstanding testimony to this truth is afforded by the career of T. E. Lawrence—"Lawrence of Arabia"—who was at one and the same time soldier, writer, and politician, and also one of the most singular personalities of his time.

The vivid portrayal of life that characterizes the English biography is also to be found in the travel books written by a nation of globe-trotters. Hardly a year passes that does not see the publication of a first-rate travel book, like those written by the youthful Peter Fleming (who went from Pekin to Kashmir) and the courageous Freya Stark, who visited the harems and fortresses of the Hadhramaut. Earlier still

Stella Benson made adventurous journeys in the Far East, and the daughter of the great Lord Birkenhead, Lady Eleanor Smith, even if she stayed at home, did so merely in order to share the life of the gipsies who are the heroes and heroines of her novels. The days are long past when women who sought danger and adventure were deemed eccentric. In this, as in other aspects of life, the Englishwoman has achieved equality with her menfolk—an equality that had already for long been accorded to her in the sphere of literature. To-day women occupy a high place in the English literary world, even as in the past Jane Austen and the sisters Brontë. Nowhere else in the world do women write so much and so well. Virginia Woolf, Katherine Mansfield, Edith Sitwell, Sheila Kaye Smith, Elizabeth Russell, Margaret Kennedy, Rebecca West, Enid Bagnold— these are names of which modern English literature is justly proud. No limitations are set to the woman writer, who is no longer content to be merely the portrayer of family and social life and to squander her talents in small and laborious compositions. Margaret Irwin has added several outstanding books to the shelves that contain England's historical fiction, and a woman, Dorothy Sayers, is the most brilliant of modern English writers of detective stories. Moreover, it was a woman who was responsible for one of the greatest literary sensations—indeed, scandals—of recent years in England when she dared to depict the tragedy of a homosexual girl. Although the law courts are no longer under the compulsion of the strict Victorian code of morals, they nevertheless prohibited the sale of Miss Radclyffe Hall's "The Well of Loneliness."

Notwithstanding its vast output, the book production of England does not appear to be sufficient to meet the demand. Apart from American books that are assured in advance of a second home in England, there is hardly a book published abroad that is of the slightest interest to the English reader that does not appear in an English translation. The World War was hardly over before the works of Keyserling, Spengler, Emil Ludwig, Feuchtwanger, and Thomas Mann were translated into English. If translations are added to the home production of books it is impossible to arrive at any other conclusion than that the English are the greatest readers in the modern world. Additional evidence in support of this conclusion is also to be found in the public and private libraries in London as well as in the Book Societies, that often buy up the first two or three editions of a new book, with the result that it only makes its appearance on the bookstalls in its fourth edition. Even wealthy people in England make use of the circulating libraries such as the "Times Book Club" or the "London Library," which have so many subscribers that they are able to supply at a low rate of subscription any book that is called for—and to supply it in good condition. An extraordinary demand has to be met by these circulating libraries at the week-end, when not only tennis racquets and golf-clubs but also books are taken into the country.

The children also are greater readers than might seem possible in view of their open-air life. England possesses vast libraries of children's books suited to every taste, whether it be for adventure, natural history, fairy tales, or humorous nonsense. Children of ten years of age are the owners of shelves full of books. Moreover, there are also humorous children's newspapers that have a far wider circulation than on the Continent.

It is obviously impossible that in a country where everyone reads there should not be a great deal of second-rate literature. The typist who takes a novel with her to her office is no more a connoisseur of literature than is the old lady who falls asleep by her fireside book in hand. The show windows of the cheap bookshops and the counters of the railway bookstalls reveal how great is the sale for novels with sentimental titles or melodramatic dust covers. The Englishman who spends his working days in his office and his Sundays in cultivating his garden seems to be seized every now and then by an imperative desire to read a murder story. It is therefore not surprising that the demand for "thrillers" should continue unabated in Edgar Wallace's native land. This demand is only equalled by that for sentimental love stories. The broad masses of the English population will, nevertheless, not tolerate an indecent story, above all when it is in print. The Church and Puritanism have spoilt their taste for such things.

English bookshops contain less real literature in the narrower sense of the term than the leading Paris and Berlin bookshops. A large part of English book production is devoted to sport, whether it be the almost scientific literature of golf and angling or the pleasures and pains of hunting, climbing, and riding. A similar interest is shown in the breeding of animals from horses down to gold fishes, and in the cultivation of flowers and the lay-out of gardens. Every Englishman cultivates and loves his garden, which, if he be wealthy, he will lay out in accordance with the principles of that art of garden design that is looked upon by England as one of the finest products of its civilization. A beautiful garden calls for a beautiful house. A beautiful house demands to be furnished with silver and china, mahogany, embroidery, tapestries, and furniture. England possesses innumerable books on these subjects that usually contain splendid illustrations. For the object of the authors is not merely to give their readers information but also to educate their taste. They are indeed largely responsible for the fact that good taste in England is in very truth *good* taste.

Throughout the two centuries during which the novel in England went from triumph to triumph the drama met with another and less fortunate fate. Under Queen Elizabeth it attained to heights that it had only scaled before in ancient Greece. Within three decades of Shakespeare's death, however, Puritanism put dramatic works on its index and in 1642 even closed the theatres. The Restoration saw the theatre restored to its place in the national life, from which it has never since been evicted. Nevertheless, despite the fact that playwriting flourished in the later seventeenth and throughout the eighteenth centuries, these plays are now nearly forgotten. Decades can pass before an English producer remembers the existence of Congreve's "Way of the World" or Sheridan's "School for Scandal." Thus it is that the modern English stage lives either on Shakespeare or the plays of the day. England has no Lessing, Kleist, Hebbel, or Grillparzer, who with Goethe and Schiller form Germany's national wealth in dramatic art. At the time when the Burgtheater was the sacred temple of the German drama, England did not possess a single theatre that could be looked upon as either a moral or æsthetic academy. It was only at the end of the nineteenth century that attempts were made to bridge the deep gulf that had separated drama and literature during the reign of Queen Victoria. In the Irishman Bernard Shaw England acquired her first great dramatist since Shakespeare. The works of other contemporary playwrights are merely of passing interest and vanish into oblivion after they have been played for a few months. There is, indeed, hardly a single English producer to be found to take the risk of putting on a play that is twenty, or even ten, years old. The only exceptions are the plays of Shaw, Oscar Wilde, and Sir James Barrie, whose "Peter Pan" has become the classic Christmas play for English children.

England has indeed to pay the penalty for its refusal to subsidize its theatre. As a result the theatre is forced to become a purely capitalistic business undertaking depending for success upon its profit-earning capacity. Hence it is that a play has hardly been written before it is bandied about, like any other kind of goods that pass through many hands, before ultimately securing a buyer. If the buyer—either a private individual or a syndicate—is not convinced of the success of the play, he first produces it in the provinces or the suburbs in order to judge of its probable reception in London itself. Only when he has satisfied himself on this point does he take the risk of hiring an expensive West End theatre where the success or failure of the piece will be decided once and for all. According to whether it runs for a week or a year, the producer is either a made man or bankrupt. His caution is, therefore, hardly to be wondered at.

The industrialization of the English theatre has obliged it to depend for its livelihood upon light entertainment and stars whose names are more familiar to the public than those of the playwrights. A dramatist is not even accorded the title of poet in England and must content himself with that of playwright. Nevertheless, within the limits set to his art, great demands are made upon a playwright's skill. He must be a master of the technique of the theatre and of dialogue. He must never forget that the London public will not suffer boredom; that it demands to be entertained and not taught; that it prefers to be made to laugh rather than to cry. It is for these reasons that witty and daring comedy, especially society comedy, is far more popular than either a tragedy or a problem play. What the English theatre thus loses in profundity it makes up in liveliness. The plays may have little lasting value; their attractiveness and interest for the playgoer of the day is beyond all praise. Darkness follows upon fireworks. Nevertheless, the heavens are lit up the moment a rocket soars upwards. The light given may not be powerful enough to illuminate the darkest depths of the human soul and human passions. It is, however, strong enough to reveal a picture of our times, of our social and sexual life, of our vanities and snobbery. Somerset Maugham and the more superficial but brilliant Noel Coward will never want audiences. In the person of Noel Coward the theatre approaches the music-hall that occupies such a large place in the amusements of England. Anyone who is fond of this form of entertainment can be certain at any time of getting his money's worth at the London revues with their nonsensical mixture of first-rate acting, singing, and dancing.

At the same time, it would be a mistake to imagine that England has wholly neglected serious drama. Even as it is impossible to judge the English Press by the sensational papers, so also the theatre as a whole must not be judged by the plays that fill the box offices. In comparison with the English literary world the theatre is little receptive of foreign influences. Ibsen, Tchekoff, and Pirandello, but not Strindberg, Björnson, and Hauptmann, have found a second home there. Shakespeare, on the other hand, is honourably housed in the Old Vic in London, while annual festivals are held at Stratford-on-Avon and Malvern at which Shakespeare's and Bernard Shaw's plays are produced. Nor must the Repertory Theatres of Birmingham, Liverpool, etc., that have done so much for the cause of drama in England, be forgotten. Nevertheless, the provinces are still, as formerly, dependent upon London, which sends them its plays by means of touring companies. There are no towns in England like Dresden or Munich to rival London as the centre of English theatrical life. Hence London is the abiding home of the most popular and most talented actors and actresses, like Charles Laughton, Leslie Howard, Leslie Henson, John Gielgud, Sybil Thorndike, Peggy Ashcroft, Diana Cooper, and above all Marie Tempest.

The cultural renaissance experienced by England during the past decade has also made itself apparent in the theatrical world. Before the War London could not be compared with Paris, Berlin, or Vienna as a centre of dramatic art. To-day it is a theatrical city of outstanding importance. Whatever may be thought of its taste in plays, there is no denying the fact that the world follows London's lead in this matter. What was formerly a puritanical and Victorian wilderness blossoms to-day with new life that is nurtured from many sources. London "First Nights" have once again become great occasions whose social brilliance must not be allowed to blind the onlooker to the obvious love of the theatre that animates the audience. It is because the English theatre does not aim at being more than a mirror of the times that it has been so successful in holding the attention of the public. Despite the competition of the cinema, England has not forgotten its theatre.

The service thus rendered by the English theatre is all the greater, because the present-day English films can no more be compared with those of the immediate post-War years. In those days America and Germany supplied the films that were shown on English screens, whilst English films were beneath contempt. Although the domination of Hollywood has not been wholly done away with, England has begun to liberate itself from foreign thraldom. An English film industry is in the making at Denham and Elstree, whose productions, such as "Henry VIII," "Rembrandt," "Sanders of the River," and "The Scarlet Pimpernel," are already beginning to turn an importing into an exporting country for films. Everything goes to prove that this development will proceed rapidly and that the day is not far distant when England will be counted among the great film-producing countries of the world. It is indeed astonishing that a country like England, which does not lack either money or dramatic talent, should have taken so long to recognize the propagandist and educational importance of the film for its empire. A Northcliffe of the film industry would not have allowed such an opportunity to remain unused for so long a time. He would not have looked on passively while the Dominions, through the lack of English films, were subjected to the influence of foreign, and, above all, American, film propaganda. Although England has awakened belatedly to the danger, it has nevertheless done so soon enough to be able to make up for the opportunities missed during the past years.

If London owes its pre-eminent position as a musical and operatic centre to the self-sacrifice of its millionaires, English science is no less indebted to their generosity. Nevertheless, even in such a generous nation as the English, who maintain great hospitals by voluntary contributions, the automobile millionaire Lord Nuffield created a great sensation by his gift of two millions for medical research. His gift came at the very moment when English medical science had begun to free itself from the old-fashioned methods that encumbered its path, as also that of the hospital organization, notwithstanding the existence of great doctors and surgeons. A similar development has taken place in the chemical industry, which was controlled by Germany before the War. Out of small beginnings Imperial Chemicals has been built up into a world-wide organization that is of the greatest importance to England for military reasons. Chemistry, like medicine, has gladly absorbed the trained minds that have come to it from Germany in recent years. In other branches of natural science

England needs no assistance from abroad in order to take her place as a leader among the nations. The biologists Huxley and Haldane, mathematicians and astronomers like Eddington and Jeans, and Lord Rutherford, who split the atom, are names that prove that England is second to none in these sciences. It is not by chance that the Royal Society, founded in 1662, has maintained its high standing throughout the centuries.

It would therefore obviously be a mistake to allow England's political and commercial greatness to obscure its cultural activities. Despite the lack of interest in intellectual pursuits shown by the average Englishman, England to-day as formerly is a home of art and science. Nowadays, when the numbers of those devoting themselves to intellectual pursuits are increasing annually, there is no longer any foundation for the accusation formerly brought against England of a want of culture. Above all, it is the youngest generation who are beginning to weary of a one-sided pre-occupation with sport and business and to demand their share in the great intellectual activities of the age. The artistic, literary, and scientific life of England is not moribund. Notwithstanding the powerful restrictive influence of tradition, it flows steadily onwards. Prudery has also become a thing of the past. The young men and women of England are perhaps less muscular and rosy-cheeked than their predecessors. Nevertheless, they are far superior to them in delicacy of feeling, æsthetic taste, and the critical faculty. Only the future can tell whether anxious politicians who think they see signs of decadence in the young generation are justified in their belief.

CHAPTER IX

SPORT AND SOCIETY

IT is a singular paradox that the Englishman is temperamentally silent and loves society, retires into the depths of the country only to fill his house with guests, and spares himself no exertion in his pursuit of pleasure, notwithstanding his almost passionate love of ease and comfort. All this, too, despite his self-sufficiency. Even among the less wealthy classes the English like to have their friends about them and if possible in their own homes. It was only in the post-War years that it became customary to entertain in restaurants. No matter in what form it is exercised, hospitality has always been and still is one of the most attractive of English characteristics.

The World War was hardly over before social life in England flourished anew like a plant brought from a dark corner into the sunlight. A victorious nation danced and drank, while its noblest sons lay buried in the soil of Flanders. The orgy gave place after a time to a social life that is not to be found anywhere else in Europe to-day. London is the centre of England's social life, and the home of English "Society," which is the only Society in Europe, with the single exception of that of Rome, that has withstood the storms of the World War. While, however, Roman Society is composed of a small circle of aristocrats and diplomatists, that of

London opens its doors to anyone possessed of money—and good manners, the only trace remaining of the exclusiveness of pre-War days, that in any case was never as great in London as in Berlin or Vienna. The Englishman has always welcomed fresh blood, and never more so than to-day, when taxation and death duties are destroying old families. The social life of London would lose its brilliance if it were to depend for its existence solely upon the holders of great names. The duchesses who formerly played so great a part in London Society are no longer able to sustain the burden. The modern Englishman, indeed, would be bored in their company. The stiff and ceremonious entertainments of former days have lost their attraction. To-day people go about to be entertained.

A brilliant and lavish social life is naturally to be found in a city where great wealth is combined with a zest for amusement and a highly developed art of hospitality. When anyone gives a ball in London, he or she invites five hundred guests, serves them with champagne, and engages the most expensive dance band. The Covent Garden Opera House at the height of the London Season affords a spectacle of dresses and jewellery that has not been seen on the Continent since pre-War days. A procession of motor-cars stretching for miles in length is to be seen in the neighbourhood of Buckingham Palace whenever the King and Queen hold a Court. A similar procession is to be met with on the roads leading to Ascot when the most fashionable race-meeting of the London Season is in progress. If to this there is added the crowds that throng the luxurious hotels and restaurants of London with their cabarets and gala nights, Cowes Week, Founder's Day at Eton on June 4th, and the Highland Gatherings and Balls in Scotland, it becomes easy to understand why England and London claim to be the greatest amusement resorts in the world. Paris, which formerly rivalled London in this respect, has long since been beaten in the race. A comparison between the social life of Paris and London serves to show unmistakably how poor France has become and how rich England has remained.

At the same time one and a half million unemployed in England suffer the pangs of hunger and millions of the poorer classes live less happy lives than their equals on the Continent. Brilliance and shabbiness, wealth and poverty live as neighbours in England. Nevertheless, the contrast is not found intolerable. The Labour Party may make use of the illustrations in the *Tatler* and the *Bystander* at election times in order to cast obloquy upon the idle rich. The broad masses of the people, nevertheless, look upon "Society" as part of England's historic heritage. A fashionable marriage brings together hundreds of poor onlookers before the church door who go home happy if they have caught a glimpse of the bride. The typist, whose duties forbid her from viewing the scene in person, consoles herself for her disappointment by studying the photographs of the ceremony that appear in the newspapers. Reflected glory is better than no glory.

In the eyes of the uninitiated, social life in London takes on the appearance of a motley crowd of revellers lacking cohesion and purpose. In reality, it is organized and arranged in such a meticulous manner that the social year has its calendar like the Gregorian year of 365 days.

The chief difference consists in the fact that the former begins in spring, when the London Season reaches its height. There is an historical explanation for this singular custom of holding the Season in spring-time. Winter is the hunting season. Since nobody wished to forego the delights of hunting London was forced to postpone its Season until the spring of the year. Hence it is that the wealthy classes spend the wet and foggy winter months in the country and only return to London when the flowers make their appearance and the trees are becoming green again. Nevertheless, London also has its share in this springtide loveliness. Its many parks and green spaces make a splendid setting for the Season's entertainments and even permit to some extent of an outdoor life. Anyone who wanders through the streets and squares of the West End on a warm spring evening will encounter numbers of young men and women in evening dress. Neither coats nor hats are necessary. For the late reveller does not step out from a warm restaurant or house into the cold of a winter's night but into the brilliant sunshine of a May morning. Only those who have been privileged to have such an experience know how lovely London can be.

For this reason there is no other city in the world where so many men and women are to be seen in the streets in full evening dress. Their appearance is the signal that the Season has begun. In the twinkling of an eye Mayfair changes its appearance. Within a few days the traffic increases to such a degree that magnificent new Rolls Royces are forced to make their first appearance at a snail's pace. Nevertheless, London's heart beats faster in a crowded space and its eyes sparkle in the radiance of thousands of many-coloured lights. The treasures of the world are exposed for sale in the fashionable and expensive shopping district of Bond Street. Theatreland also provides a brilliant spectacle. The pavements before the theatres are crowded with men in evening-dress and women in silks and velvets. No sooner has the curtain fallen than the crowd moves on to the fashionable restaurants and night resorts, where Italian head-waiters contrive to find places where no place exists. Time as well as space is an expensive commodity at this time of night. England, where so much drink is consumed, is at least legally "half dry." After midnight or two o'clock in the morning at the latest no alcohol may be served in even the most luxurious of London restaurants and night clubs. A waiter takes the glass from the hand of the guest five minutes before the legal closing time in the freest country in the world. If the guests are still thirsty they must content themselves with Apollinaris, or else be prepared to pay the exorbitant charges demanded by the proprietor of an illegal night club threatened nightly by a police raid. The golden age of night clubs was in the years immediately following upon the World War, when young men and women amused themselves by getting arrested. Nowadays this sport has ceased to be fashionable and a merry company fleeing from the menace of soda-water will seek refuge and stronger refreshment in a friend's house, where they can continue their revelry safely and less expensively than in a night club. Notwithstanding the fact that the restaurateurs and hotel keepers have time and again protested against these police regulations, their complaints have gone unheeded by the authorities. A feeling of social justice forbids the Government to distinguish in this sense between the West End and the East End, where the closing hour has proved an immense blessing. The rich shall not have their champagne—at least publicly— during the hours in which the poor are forbidden to drink. Equality before the law must be preserved even at the cost of London's night life in so far as it is carried on in public.

The London Season lasts from May to the end of July. These are the months in which the great Society balls as well as the Courts and Ascot races take place. Only those who are invited into the "Royal Enclosure" at Ascot are truly members of the upper ten thousand. For this reason Ascot is the Mecca of those who wish to rise in the social scale—the "climbers," as England calls this well-known class of people. A still smaller circle forms "Society" at the regatta at Cowes, where is to be found the most exclusive club in the world—the Royal Yacht Squadron. Only owners of private yachts are eligible for membership and only then when their personal character is beyond question. Cowes Week brings the Season to its close. Its beginning was heralded by the opening of the Royal Academy and of the Grand Opera season at Covent Garden that is chiefly devoted to the works of Verdi and Wagner. The Opera is not only a great artistic but also an equally important social event, and as such of great splendour. If anywhere to-day, it is in Covent Garden that it is possible to forget that a new age began with the World War that has nothing in common with the age of Edward VII and Wilhelm II. In Covent Garden Time has stood still.

Although the London Season still continues throughout July, it has already passed its zenith when the
heat begins to make itself felt oppressively at the last
balls and entertainments. Once more the country comes
into its own, with the result that London in August is a
dead city. Country life, on the other hand, becomes
increasingly lively with the beginning of the shooting
season on August 12th. The heart of every *bon vivant*
as well as of every lover of shooting beats faster at the
mention of this date on which the Scottish and Yorkshire moors—the home of the grouse—become the
centre of social life. Moreover, the day is not far distant
when hunting will begin again. Meanwhile London
sleeps its summer sleep until the middle of October,
when it awakes to the so-called "Little Season," which,
with its dances, first nights, and concerts, is a foretaste of
the Season that is to come. Christmas sees another
migration to the country, that is followed in January by
another return to London for a sort of rehearsal for the
Season that begins three months later. In comparison
with the Continent, however, where social life attains
its greatest intensity during the winter months, the
winter in London is—socially speaking—a time of rest.

Such, then, is the annual social round of those
pleasure-seekers who possess sufficient wealth to be able
to dance, hunt, and bet at race-meetings. The making of
the full round is obligatory. Anyone who absents himself or pursues it half-heartedly is soon forgotten. The
duties and responsibilities of Society hostesses are too
numerous to enable them to bear in mind those persons
who do not constantly recall themselves to their
memory by their presence. In this connection it is not

sufficient merely to leave cards—a custom that is in any case falling into desuetude. The tempo of social life in London nowadays is too fast to afford the younger generations time for making formal calls. Moreover, it must also be remembered that even the wealthy classes work in England and therefore find the day hardly long enough to enable them to keep pace both with their business and social engagements. The only places the weary Englishman can find in which to rest himself are the Clubs, which he visits for that purpose rather than in search of entertainment.

A Club is therefore not looked upon with disfavour if its atmosphere is one of boredom and if its members sit about on chairs far removed from each other, like islands upon which it is forbidden for anyone except the owner to land. Two Englishmen may sit side by side at lunch in a Club for decades without knowing each other. Nowhere is the right to individual privacy more carefully guarded than in London's Clubs. In order that the peace and privacy of the men may not be disturbed by their intrusion, women, who in any case have their own Clubs, are excluded or only admitted on special days. The Englishman's Club is his temple, in which he refreshes himself after the labours of the day either alone or in the company of a few friends : a fact that does not prevent the Clubs from being the scenes of weighty deliberations and important decisions that have vitally affected England's destiny. In the eyes of the Labour and Liberal Parties the Carlton Club is the home of Tory conspirators, while the members of the Carlton in their turn look with suspicion upon the National Liberal Club. In addition to the political Clubs there are social Clubs, like White's and Bucks', naval and military and professional Clubs, the Royal Automobile Club and the Athenæum—the Mecca of the English world of letters. Each Club confers a distinctive imprint upon its members, whose visiting-cards bearing the name of the Club reveal their owners' political sympathies and social standing. In conjunction with the Public School and the University the Club is the training-ground of the "gentleman," who is judged in England not by his manners in women's society but by his behaviour in association with his fellow men. Exclusion from a Club is therefore tantamount to sentence of death in a social sense. Nevertheless, "Clubland" is no longer what it was in its great days during the last century. A reason for this is that membership of a good Club is expensive.

Anyone who wishes to take part in the social life of England must indeed be prepared to spend money lavishly. London spares itself no trouble for its sons and their guests if only they are able to pay for it. Even English cooking, that was formerly the dread of every gourmet, can no longer be compared with that of pre-War days. First-rate food is to be obtained to-day in the great houses, restaurants, and hotels. This improvement is due to foreigners and, above all, to the French and the Italians. The French taught the English the art of cooking, while Italian managers have raised London hotels and restaurants to the Continental level. For the Englishman is not by nature a good cook and is content with his excellent beef and mutton without troubling himself about the finer points of the culinary art. A classical example of this is Simpson's Restaurant in the Strand, where English cooks show what they can do.

The restaurants in Soho, on the other hand, and also the luxury hotels in Mayfair, are under foreign management. If Soho and the West End are too dear for anyone's pocket, his state is indeed parlous. Nothing remains to him except the ordinary lunch and the ordinary dinner, whose courses are only to be distinguished from one another by the fact that each is more unattractive and less skilfully prepared than the other. In addition to the small restaurants, there are the great mass-eating-places that are filled to the last available seat despite the fact that the food is cooked and despatched with machine-like rapidity. These are the restaurants frequented by the less well-to-do classes and to which they also go after the theatre. London has no cafés like Berlin or Paris where an evening's entertainment may be brought to its close. Nor has it many cheap dance-halls. The night life of London is an affair for the rich rather than the poor. The streets of this gigantic city are empty by midnight. It is only on special occasions such as Derby night, Boat Race night, a great national event like the King's Jubilee or a General Election that the Londoner sacrifices his sleep in order to celebrate. London knows no ordinary nights, but only great nights, whose effect is all the more overwhelming because the seldom expressed emotion of a nation makes itself felt beneath the exemplary discipline of the crowds —and never more so than when England is in peril or has triumphantly emerged from danger. Hence Armistice night was an unforgettable event in English history. A generation before, the relief of Mafeking occasioned a similar demonstration that has left its mark on the English language in the form of the word "mafficking."

SPORT AND SOCIETY

On such occasions money and class differences vanish. Beggars and millionaires dance together round the statue of Eros in Piccadilly Circus united in the knowledge that they are one and all England's sons. Nobody knows England who has not lived through such a night. It is then that the sources from which England has drawn her strength throughout the centuries are clearly seen. Time and again England's destiny has been decided on London's pavements.

The crowds that thronged the streets on the night of Edward VIII's abdication filled them again on King George VI's Coronation day. The Coronation afforded England an opportunity of enhancing the London Season by a great national and imperial celebration. It seems hardly possible with the eventful day May 12 in mind to believe that the Coronation could have been more splendid if Edward VIII had been the central figure rather than his less spectacular and more reserved brother. London certainly had its money's worth; and especially the London that has been described above as the city of great Society entertainments. For the women and girls of England the Coronation was a great event, and for none more so than for those fortunate enough to be presented at Court—an unforgettable day. It is only with her presentation that the young Englishwoman enjoys full membership of English Society. Then—and only then—does the debutante come of age. Moreover, presentation at Court is by no means restricted to the daughters of the nobility and the upper ten thousand.

While the social life of Italy and France centres round the young married woman, it is the young unmarried woman who occupies the foremost place during the London Season. A debutante—known for short as "deb"—has hardly "put her hair up" before her portrait appears in the newspapers and society journals. Great balls are given in her honour, and this young girl, who only left school a few months previously, is feted like a queen. Her hey-day only lasts for one or at the most two Seasons. A new generation has by then sprung up, and the debutante of yesterday leaves the stage to disappear as an "ex-deb" in the broad stream of Society, from which she does not again emerge until her engagement is announced in the newspapers—a custom that takes the place in England of the engagement notices that are sent privately by Continental families to their friends. It is a natural corollary to this custom that marriages in England should be celebrated in circumstances of greater publicity than in Germany, where only the immediate relatives are present at the ceremony. In England every fashionable wedding attracts crowds of curious onlookers apart from the friends and relatives who have been invited to attend the ceremony. The object of each of these sightseers is to catch a glimpse of the bride as she leaves the church under a shower of rice or confetti. This custom of showering confetti on a bride explains why the streets are often strewn with it in London, where carnival is only known by hearsay.

The bride leaves the church on the arm of her husband. She does not enter it with him. It is an English custom that bride and bridegroom do not meet on their wedding-day until they stand before the altar. Shortly before the beginning of the ceremony the bridegroom and his "best man" take their places before the altar to await the coming of the bride, who enters the church on the arm of her nearest male relative, usually her father or brother, who gives the bride away to her husband and thereby publicly signalizes the fact that she has left her own for another family. The clergyman then begins the marriage service. At a sign from him the "best man" hands the wedding-ring to the bridegroom, who places it on the fourth finger of his bride's left hand. He himself does not receive or wear a wedding-ring. The ceremony itself bears a close resemblance to the German Lutheran service.

The instant the young couple make their appearance at the door of the vestry, where they have signed their names in the Church register, the music loses its spiritual character. Wedding marches by Wagner and Mendelssohn take the place of anthems and sacred music. The young couple proceed down the aisle attended by bridesmaids and pages to the accompaniment of these festal strains. From the church they drive to the house of the bride's parents, where a reception is held that lasts until the bride and bridegroom depart for their honeymoon. For the German *Polterabend* is unknown in England, where its place is taken by "farewell" parties given separately by bride and bridegroom to their most intimate friends on the evening before the wedding.

The wedding reception serves a more practical purpose than that of affording their friends an opportunity of offering the newly married couple their best wishes. The display of wedding presents in the reception rooms is of equal importance. So numerous are these presents in the case of a fashionable Society wedding that several rooms are often required for their display. Wedding presents are of far greater importance in England than on the Continent, and are expected of everyone who receives an invitation to the ceremony. These presents are intended to—and in fact do—assist the newly married couple to furnish their home. One uncle gives china, another glass, a grandmother supplies the household linen, and other relatives and friends contribute their share towards the furnishing of the house down to the cellar and the kitchen. For this reason it is not uncommon for a young couple with a big circle of friends and relatives to send lists of their household requirements to the shops, and to inform the would-be donors that if they will inquire at such and such shop they will be told what gifts would be most acceptable. The custom may seem curious. Nevertheless, it has the great advantage of preventing the giving of useless presents and of duplicates. Duplicates can in any case be exchanged at the great London shops, like Asprey's. As in so many other aspects of English life, so also in this aspect, utilitarianism takes the place of sentimentality. For the same reason cheques are especially welcome as wedding presents.

The custom of showering wedding presents upon newly wedded couples is common to all classes—excepting only the poorest—in the population. Hence bridal couples belonging to even less wealthy families often receive presents to the value of many hundreds of pounds. In this fashion England makes up for the absence of the Continental custom of a bridal dowry and the furnishing of the newly married couple's home by the bride's parents. According to the traditional Anglo-Saxon point of view, it is the bridegroom's duty to provide for the material welfare of his future wife and family even down to the furnishing of their home. A young bride therefore enters on married life with only her trousseau. Recent changes in the economic structure of society have naturally contributed to deprive this principle of its practical validity. Nowadays a wealthy father often gives his daughter a house, a personal allowance, or a marriage settlement. It is nevertheless still exceptional for parents to make a heavy financial sacrifice during their lifetime in order to give their daughters private incomes. Moreover, families that look upon the law of primogeniture as sacrosanct usually make small financial provision for their daughters. This fact, coupled with the young Englishman's dislike of mixing up affairs of the heart with those of the purse, has brought it about that marrying for money alone is still a rare occurrence in England, and that the least well-off girl is able to make a great marriage. The French family lawyer who arranges marriages between persons of equal wealth is unknown in England.

England still holds fast to its ideal of a marriage for love and is therefore prepared to overlook class differences to a greater extent than is even now customary on the Continent. A beautiful girl is always eligible. The wealth of England has naturally made it easier to ignore material considerations when it comes to a question of marriage. Many Englishmen can earn sufficient at an early age to be able to marry the girl of their choice, even if she is possessed of nothing more than what she stands up in. Nevertheless, the heart would hardly seem to be a wise guide in this matter. Divorce is assuming alarming proportions in England, and it is often the romantic marriages that end in disaster. How many marriages end in the divorce court while the young wife still bears the title of "bride"? Nor is this any contradiction in terms. Unlike her German sister, an Englishwoman is a "bride" from the day of her marriage until the end of the first year of married life. Before her marriage she bears the title of "fiancée," while her betrothed is styled "fiancé," and only bears the title of "bridegroom" for a few weeks before and after the wedding. Stern moralists need not therefore be shocked if they read in the English newspapers that Lord So-and-so has gone to Nice with his "bride." Of all young women who are to be found on the Riviera the English brides are the most married.

The brilliant and luxurious Society of London is saved by its old traditions from snobbishness and a vulgar display of wealth. Not the newly rich but the old families give Society its standards of taste and behaviour; and these families have been successful in keeping English Society free from the worst features of American Society. The social, like the political, world in London believes to-day that it has nothing to learn from foreigners, and even that the rest of the world could go to school in England with advantage to itself. Even the domination of Paris fashions no longer exists as in pre-War days, when fashionable Englishwomen bought their clothes in Paris alone. It is true that the Englishman in contrast to his feminine counterpart never thought of dressing himself in accordance with foreign taste. To-day as formerly Savile Row dictates the fashion in male clothing to the world. Its tailors have made the Englishman the best dressed man alive. An English suit is more manly in appearance than that worn in Latin countries and without the too broad shoulders that are fashionable in America. The English tailor reproaches his German counterpart with turning out his clients as if they had emerged from a band-box. An Englishman must never appear as if he had just left his tailor or spent an hour before the looking-glass. No well-dressed Englishman must convey an impression of vanity. Hence the English suit—well cut though it must be—must never appear brand-new and its wearer must seem to be unaware of its existence. The great dandies of the past were actually in the habit of having their new suits rubbed down with emery-paper in order to take away their newness. Just as the manners of an Englishman must be easy and natural in order to be good, so his suit must not fit him too closely and give him the appearance of being self-conscious. The same naturalness that characterizes eating and drinking must also characterize the art of dressing. A man and his clothes must fit each other as if they had grown together rather than come from a tailor's workshop. It has already been pointed out above that English should be spoken as it were "casually." Similarly, clothes should be worn with an air of carelessness.

An Englishman's wardrobe can be divided into three sections. In the first hang the evening clothes—tails and dinner-jacket—usually known as "white tie" or "black tie." If the tail-coat is not worn to-day with the same frequency as formerly, it is still the correct wear in women's society. An Englishman therefore wears his tail-coat when he goes to the opera or a "first night" or when he dines in a fashionable hotel or restaurant. He

invariably wears it at a dance. Apart from male gatherings, the dinner-jacket is only permissible at small or
private parties and is therefore chiefly worn at home.
For it is the custom for well-bred English people to
dress for dinner even when no guests are to be present.
In recent days a very decorative green or dark blue velvet
dinner jacket that is worn with a soft white silk shirt
has become fashionable.

In comparison with evening dress day clothes
permit their wearer a wider choice. The suit itself is
almost invariably blue, grey, or brown. The choice of
socks and ties to wear with it is left wholly to the owner's
discretion. Black shoes are customarily worn in towns,
while brown is the colour for sporting and country
shoes. No well-dressed Englishman ever wears brown or
yellow shoes with a blue suit. Since the War overcoats
are usually dark blue in colour for winter wear, grey for
summer, and brown for country use. The fawn-coloured
summer overcoat that is so much worn in Germany is
unknown in England. A green felt hat like those worn
in music-hall skits on German habits is looked upon as
impossible for town wear. Germans are also laughed at
in England for wearing hats that are too small and that
balance precariously on the top of the head. An English
hat, on the other hand, covers the head so completely
that it almost rests on the top of the ears. In common
with the green felt hat the straw hat, despite the efforts
of Edward VIII, has also gone out of fashion, and an
Englishman covers his head in summer and winter
either with a top-hat, a bowler hat, or with a grey or
black felt hat. The latter has also become fashionable for
evening wear and has largely superseded the top-hat

for this purpose. Although top-hats are still worn more frequently in England than on the Continent, they are no longer as common as they were before the War. It is a natural result of the less formal character of modern fashions that the morning coat is quickly following the frock-coat into oblivion. Anybody who is invited to a luncheon-party nowadays appears in either a lounge suit or a short black coat with grey striped trousers. The habit of carrying an umbrella in all weathers is a peculiarity of English life. No well-dressed man would go out in England even on a fine day without an umbrella in his hand. If it rains the umbrella will nevertheless remain unopened and its owner will summon a taxi to prevent him from getting his feet wet. Goloshes are never worn in England by civilians any more than by officers. To distinguish officers from civilians takes a trained eye. Uniform is only worn by officers in England when on duty, and never in the streets, at the theatre, or in society. Court functions form the sole exception to this universal rule. At all other entertainments, from private dinner-parties to great balls, the English officer appears in evening dress. In Scotland, however, he, like the civilian, wears the extraordinarily picturesque national costume. Nevertheless, it takes a Scottish skin to be able to wear the kilt in all weathers.

The moment the Englishman leaves the town for the country he changes his style of dress. Nothing appears to him to be more wanting in taste than to wear town clothes in the country. Hence his black shoes are exchanged for brown and his ordinary trousers for grey flannels or plus fours. (The name "plus fours" derives from the fact that this form of breeches is supposed to hang down four inches over the knees.) He puts on a pull-over or a waistcoat made out of the same tweed as his coat. Soft coloured collars matching the shirt have already begun to supersede the stiff white collar for town wear. In any case this latter is never worn in the country, where an Englishman likes to be as free as possible in his movements, even at the sacrifice of being well-dressed. A man who seeks to be well-dressed in the country is lacking in that sense of fitness that is the secret of the well-dressed man. The English have an extraordinarily fine and highly developed sense of what clothing should or should not be worn on different occasions. An Englishman always knows when he must be well dressed and when he can put on his oldest clothes. He seems to know by instinct when a weather-beaten hat and a stained mackintosh look more appropriate from an æsthetic standpoint than the best and most correctly cut clothes. Similarly, the Englishwoman leaves high heels and dark dresses behind her in the town and wears tweeds and jerseys for country wear. It is not the least of the many charms of English country life that it affords both men and women an opportunity of wearing such sensible and comfortable clothes.

The same is also true of sport. An Englishman would sooner give up his day's sport than appear in the wrong clothing. Nobody therefore plays tennis or golf without changing into the appropriate clothes. Sport is an Englishman's recreation and requires for its proper enjoyment that his body should be able to move about freely. It is by the clothing worn for sport that the underlying purpose of English sport is revealed—to serve as a recreation rather than a means to fame. For the same reason the English jealously guard the amateur nature of their sports and make a very clear line of demarcation between professionals and amateurs. It is with suspicion that the Englishman views sport in other countries, where he believes that it has become a profession rather than an amusement. Moreover, whenever possible the Englishman does not confine himself to a single sport but plays tennis and golf, rides and fishes, boxes and hunts. Only thus—thinks the Englishman— does every part of the body attain its due share of exercise. The achievement of this aim seems more important in his eyes than the acquisition of innumerable prizes and cups. It was for this reason that England's pride was not seriously injured by the poor show made by the English competitors at the Olympic Games. Their defeat was ascribed in England to the highly specialized training of their foreign rivals. In English eyes specialization of this kind is not sport.

England, indeed, is much concerned over the growing commercialization of its sport. Although professionalism is tolerated in the boxing world, it is looked upon with disfavour in that of football. It is contrary to the English conception of sport that the championship should be won by the club that is wealthy enough to purchase the best players. Cricket is looked upon as a cleaner sport than football simply because it is so far free from this vice. Football betting has taken on dimensions that place it in the same category with betting on horse-racing and boxing. England looks with disfavour on a development that is causing the number of the spectators to increase by a hundredfold whilst that of the actual players is on the decrease. It is because England expects each of her sons to prove his worth on the playing-field that it is determined to put an end to this decrease at all costs.

English sport is intended to serve not only as a means of physical training but also of character-building. It is on the playing fields that the Englishman learns fair play and self-control—the two foundations of the English State. English sport is also organized like a political institution in as much as every branch has a claim upon a clearly defined season of the year. Summer is devoted to cricket, tennis, flat racing, yachting, and polo. Winter is the season for football, steeplechasing, fox-hunting, hockey, and rowing. Only golf, which originated in Scotland, is not confined to any particular season of the year, because—at least, so the English say —it is impossible in Scotland to distinguish between summer and winter. The result of this seasonal division of sport is that no month in the year is without its particular sport and that English arms and legs have no cause to complain of idleness unless their owners are devotees of one sport alone. Similarly, as a result of the division of sporting life between the various seasons of the year the great sporting events of the year, such as the Boat Race, the Derby, the Grand National, and the Cup Final are looked upon by the English people as national events. As the French celebrate July 14th and the Fascists the March on Rome, so England celebrates its great sporting events. These days are true popular holidays that every employer respects, as, for example, when his employees ask him for a holiday to visit the Derby. On these occasions the most silent nation in the world becomes a nation of shouters that gather together in their hundreds of thousands, forget their habitual reserve, and behave like a nation of school-boys. Sport—and not the theatre—is the refuge of those who seek to escape from the deadly monotony that envelops the daily life of the ordinary Englishman. If now and then a race-meeting or a game of football affords a means of forgetfulness, poverty and misery are accepted as an inevitable accompaniment of daily life. Even the criminal world has its sporting fans who are not solely concerned to win money.

The sports grounds of England are also its gambling dens. No matter how level-headed an Englishman may be, the love of adventure runs in his veins and urges him to seek the favours of the Goddess of Chance. Hence it is that the Law, which forbids gambling, affords an outlet for the Englishman's speculative instinct by permitting betting. Neither the Church nor Puritanism has been able to destroy this passion, and they have therefore contented themselves with diverting it into the relatively harmless channel of betting on sporting events. Nevertheless, the reports of bankruptcy proceedings show that betting has its victims. Moreover, women are no less passionately devoted to betting than men. Not only the porter but also the servant-girl puts a shilling on the Derby, while the young woman of fashion risks her entire dress-allowance at smart race-meetings. In view of the strength of this passion it is only astonishing that it has not led to greater evils and that the English, despite all exceptions to the contrary, have sufficient self-control to keep their passion within bounds. It should be added that in the clubs stakes are played for at bridge and poker that Continental card players have long since been unable to afford.

Notwithstanding the close connection between sport and betting, the English have not lost their sincere love of sport for its own sake. Sport in England is not a mere adjunct to life. It is an integral part of life itself, without which it would cease to be worth the living. It belongs as much to the life of women as to that of men. An Englishman can safely aver that he is not interested in politics, art, or even making money. Let him, however, declare that he is not interested in sport—every true Englishman will treat him with the contumely which, in his opinion, is his desert. Something—the Englishman says to himself in this case—is wrong somewhere and it will be best to leave the queer fellow to himself. The gulf is too deep to be bridged over. Thus Bernard Shaw could not have distinguished himself more sharply from his fellow-countrymen than he did by writing beneath his name in "Who's Who" under the heading "Recreations": "Everything except sport." In writing this Shaw revealed not only that he was no true Englishman but also that he was not a true Irishman. If England and Ireland have nothing else in common, they are united in a common love of hunting, racing, and betting. Dublin itself is the home of the greatest sweepstake in the world—the Irish Sweepstake —in which hundreds of thousands can be won by the holders of the lucky numbers. In the same way that England is united to Ireland by a common love of horses, it is joined to Australia by cricket, Canada by hockey, and India by polo; while South Africa and India meet in peaceful battles on the cricket pitch. In addition to democracy, the language, and the Crown, sport is another link that holds together England's world Empire. Finally, would it be inappropriate to mention the organization of the Boy Scouts founded by Lord Baden Powell, which arouses a consciousness of Empire and imperial responsibilities in the coming generations at home and overseas?

CHAPTER X

QUO VADIS, BRITANNIA?

DESPITE the fact that the wounds dealt the British Empire during the World War were not to be compared with those inflicted on France or Germany, England nevertheless suffered severely. Immense material and moral efforts were necessary to defeat Germany and to deliver England from the most serious danger that had threatened it since the Napoleonic Wars. While the defeat of Germany was England's chief objective, it was not the only one. Curious as it may sound to-day, England was fighting for the ideal of creating a better world upon the ruins of the old. England itself was to be made a country "fit for heroes" to live in when they came home from the trenches, and under the banner of Democracy and the ægis of the League of Nations the era of peace upon earth was to dawn in the world at large. The fact that England failed to achieve these aims must not be allowed to throw doubt upon English idealism.

The real question is, Why did England fail to realize her aims? At the time of the Armistice England was certainly at the zenith of its power. Germany and Russia had been beaten to their knees. France was bleeding from a thousand wounds and owed an eternal debt of gratitude to its saviour. From what quarter could England's peace proposals anticipate opposition?

Moreover, England could count upon the support of the United States in its endeavour to reconstruct civilization on new foundations. Unhappily for the future destiny of Europe and the world, Clemenceau proved stronger than Lloyd George or Woodrow Wilson. The two Anglo-Saxon statesmen failed at Versailles, and with their failure the hope of a better world receded from men's vision. Behind Clemenceau and his dictated peace stood a united France with an army fully equipped for carrying on the war, while Lloyd George was dependent upon a coalition Government whose members were disunited and whose soldiers had returned to their homes. England paid heavily in those days for the fact that conscription, which had been introduced in the worst days of the War, was limited in its duration to the War itself. The British army insisted upon immediate demobilization after the Armistice. The disappearance of the British Army affected the Franco-British balance of power in a sense adverse to England for many a long day after the signing of the peace treaty. England put its signature to a treaty that was looked upon as unjust by the English people as soon as the first wave of anti-German feeling within the country itself had died away. Though England insisted that both the peace treaty itself and the Covenant of the League of Nations should be capable of revision, the League of Nations, which America refused to enter, received its death-blow at the very instant of its birth. The French army stood in the path of revision. It was their bayonets that enabled Poincaré to override England's objection to the occupation of the Ruhr— an occupation which cost France dear. With the occupation of the Ruhr and the Separatist movement in the Rhineland supported by France, English public opinion underwent a change. No longer was it a case of "Hats off to France!" Instead France was recognized as the real obstacle in the way of the reconstruction of Europe.

During the succeeding years England tried to assist Germany to recovery. At the time of the Locarno Pact it did indeed seem as if a part at least of the Treaty of Versailles might undergo revision. Germany entered the League of Nations and the allied armies were withdrawn from the Rhineland. It soon appeared, however, that Locarno, which in the words of its sponsors was intended only to be a beginning, was in reality an end. In the course of the next few years, it is true, reparation payments were suspended. Not, however, because a reasonable compromise had been attained, but because a system which had brought Europe to the verge of ruin collapsed under the weight of its own stupidity. In the same way the inter-allied war-debts policy led to nothing. It seemed as if problems which could not be mastered by human endeavour melted away of their own volition. England, nevertheless, had not yet buried its greatest hope—the hope of a general disarmament. No one can deny that the English themselves set a good example by disarming to an extent that endangered the defence of the country. Nevertheless, instead of inducing others to follow its example, England simply weakened its own influence and thereby crippled the strongest force at work in Europe in the service of international co-operation. The situation of the world would probably be different to-day if England had realized betimes that political ideals are only as powerful as the force by which they are backed.

The lack of success attending England's efforts in post-War years has not been confined to the realm of foreign politics. Four years after he had led his country to victory Lloyd George fell from power never to rise again. He was succeeded by Bonar Law, a dying man, who in his turn was succeeded by a then unknown man called Stanley Baldwin. At the same time a new and powerful force made its appearance in the English political arena. From small beginnings the Labour Party grew to such proportions that it was able—if only with the help of the Liberals—to form a Government. MacDonald, Snowden, and Henderson led a Socialist Cabinet into 10 Downing Street for the first time. Hitherto the famous house had been occupied only by Liberals and Tories. Although the fears of a Socialist Revolution were not fulfilled in the event, and the new Government proved more moderate than had been expected of it, MacDonald's first Government—and, indeed, also the second one which he formed after a brief Tory interlude—lacked effectiveness. It was during Mr. MacDonald's tenure of office that the world was confronted with the incredible spectacle of disorder in England's finances. The pound fell and with it one of the pillars which held up post-War England.

At the time of the financial crisis the English people once more showed that it is never greater than when it is threatened by danger. Not only did the nation's nerves remain perfectly steady, and thus prevent an outbreak of panic, but it forgot its internal dissensions overnight. Acting under the King's influence, the party leaders,

MacDonald and Baldwin, were the first to set the good example, and by shaking hands these erstwhile antagonists taught the English people to subordinate Party interests to the common weal. Their appeal to the patriotism of their people was not in vain. As one man England supported the National Government, which won one of the most resounding victories in English parliamentary history at the following General Election. The Labour Party was smashed. When MacDonald entered the new House of Commons he found himself confronted by a tiny Opposition composed of die-hard Socialists and Liberals. On the Government side of the House sufficient seating accommodation could not be found for the Conservative, Liberal, and Socialist members who had united under the banner of the National Government. Although Baldwin was the leader of the strongest Party, the Conservatives, he voluntarily renounced the Premiership and accepted a subordinate post in a Government led by Mr. MacDonald as Prime Minister, who had only a handful of his own supporters with him. The wildest imagination of a political novelist was surpassed by the historic event which had placed Mac-Donald at the head of what was fundamentally a Conservative Cabinet. "Red Ramsay," the Tory bogy, who had been threatened with the gallows at the time of the World War as a fanatical pacifist, had become the saviour of his native land beneath the Conservative banner.

The General Election that brought the National Government to power marks a great turning-point in English history. It was at this time that England discarded Free Trade. For generations Free Trade had been the great bone of contention in English politics. Obstinately as the Conservative protectionists had attacked the Liberal Free Traders' citadel, it had never been captured; and one of the greatest of English statesmen, Joseph Chamberlain, fell in the assault. In recent years the wind had been blowing from another quarter. England had become a Protectionist country, and with it the Empire. A new situation had been created and the world at large was forced to adapt itself to the changed conditions.

The moral effect of the General Election was equally important. The post-War years had seen a slackening of effort in England. The General Election that brought the National Government into office was the first step towards a revival and reintegration of the national forces. Looking back upon the path it had trodden since the War, England saw only a heap of ruins. The numbers of the unemployed were increasing on the Continent, in America, and within its own borders. The task of international reconciliation at which England had worked so persistently had ended in failure, even as the World Economic Conference was to prove unsuccessful. The League of Nations, to which England had attached high hopes, was rapidly losing favour in the eyes of the nations. Although the ideal of disarmament was still being pursued, no progress was being made. The world was growing weary of political and economic conferences, and refused to be taken in any longer by the formulæ by which their failure was disguised. Even Democracy, for which the War was to have made the world ready, ceased to be believed in as the only possible State form that could confer happiness on mankind. Tsarism, which England had loathed, was succeeded in Russia by a still more autocratic and far more brutal form of government. Liberal Italy had become Fascist Italy. Germany went through the same evolution. Wherever England looked, the course of events had run contrary to British ideals. The great victory of the Allies had been gambled away. Their sons had died in vain. It was therefore with feelings of bitter disappointment that England regarded these post-War years of which the best that could be said was that they had not led to another war.

The worst was, nevertheless, still to come. Germany walked out of the Disarmament Conference, which was in any case on the point of dissolution, to the accompaniment of painful convulsions. At the same time Germany also withdrew from the League of Nations. While Geneva was conferring, Japanese armies advanced into Manchukuo. It says much for England's steadfastness that even now it did not falter in its loyalty to the League of Nations. Indeed, its loyalty was greater than ever when Mussolini embarked on the conquest of Abyssinia. Supported by the influential League of Nations Union, by the Church, and by the Opposition, the English Government stood behind the League and the Negus. For their sake Sir Samuel Hoare, the Secretary of State for Foreign Affairs, was swept out of office by a whirlwind of public opinion and branded as a traitor because he had suggested that the Negus should surrender at least a part of his empire. England threw itself heart and soul into the campaign for the enforcement of sanctions against Italy, which it conducted far more on account of the League of Nations and Abyssinia than for the sake of its own imperial interests. The outcome was the most serious defeat that England has sustained for generations.

Nevertheless, as England had drawn strength for its national revival from the sterling crisis, so it derived political strength from its defeat over sanctions. The Conservative Government had been defeated by Mussolini; and the Socialist and Liberal Opposition were not backward with their reproaches. None the less, the Government managed to make capital out of its defeat. If England had laid down its arms, it was because it possessed none worthy of the name. An unarmed England, the Government said to the nation, had been left in the lurch by the League of Nations and had been defeated. The ground was well tilled and the seed took root. Germany had been responsible for the beginning of rearmament in England. Italy was now brought in to serve the same purpose of making the rate at which rearmament was proceeding and also its extent palatable to the masses of the English populace, who would not have accepted it at all in other circumstances. By this clever exploitation of his defeat, Baldwin, who is not a great statesman but a tactician of genius, won over public opinion to his side for the greatest armament programme that England has ever embarked upon in times of peace. The Conservatives were able to summon the nation to rearm without encountering opposition from the Liberals and Socialists, since it was the latter and not the Conservatives who had clamoured for war at the time of the sanctions crisis.

Since 1931 England may thus pride herself on two

great achievements. It has put itself on the road to economic prosperity by setting its house in order and by protecting its home market from foreign competition. Only the future can tell whether the new system of Protection will be successful or not. Meanwhile no doubt can at present be entertained that England is prospering economically under its new tariff system and rearmament. Despite the distressed areas and a million and a half ill-nourished unemployed, England gives the impression of being a rich country; and as such is regarded with envy not only by an impoverished Europe but also by the United States. While on the Continent rearmament preceded economic reconstruction, England adopted the opposite order. Before beginning to mechanize the Army, strengthen the Navy, and construct a vast air force, Whitehall and the City filled their purses. No matter how great may be the sacrifices that the nation is called upon to make for the sake of rearmament, it is at least able to make them with the knowledge that its resources are vast. England will in truth make any necessary sacrifice because the nation is awake to the necessity of rearmament, and because in this as in other spheres the post-War lassitude has been overcome. The England of 1937 is not the England of 1936. A new era has dawned that also reveals itself in the British Government's more forceful foreign policy.

England would not be England were its military recrudescence not allied with a diplomatic one. From the earliest times an English diplomatist was always to be found following closely behind every English army and seeking allies. England refuses to believe that even the strongest Power is really strong in isolation. On the contrary; its history has taught England how much can be made out of well-chosen allies. It is not England's generals and admirals who have won its wars, but its statesmen. Over and over again in the course of its history England has entered upon a war unprepared— but only unprepared in a military sense. Diplomatically all the mines have been laid and all the ambushes prepared. Any state that makes war on England must therefore realize not only that it is fighting against a rich nation that will stop short of no sacrifice in the hour of need, but also that behind the advancing British armies are the cleverest diplomatists in the world. In this sense England's heraldic emblem—the lion—is ill-chosen. The English nation does not fight like a lion, but like a boa-constrictor.

The more strenuously munition factories are working the more busily is the Foreign Office at work. Not that England desires to attack any country. On the contrary, England, which has nothing to gain and much to lose, looks upon peace as its highest goal. The fact that this is not a moral virtue but a matter of course for a rich country like England only makes the English desire for peace more sincere. Nevertheless, England believes to-day more strongly than at any other time since the War that it must be on its guard. For this purpose English foreign policy has divided the nations of the world into two groups: the unthinkable enemies, that is to say, those nations who could never be antagonists; and the potential enemies, that is to say, those nations with whom a war comes within the range of possibility. Among the "unthinkable enemies" England believes

that she can only place two great Powers with certainty
—France and the United States.

This is the only possible explanation of the fact
that since the War England has departed from its
historical principle that the British Navy must be
greater than any other. At the Naval Conference in
Washington, and again in London, England accepted
parity with the United States and thus conceded to
America what it had refused, in Wilhelm II's time, to
Germany. Regardless of its prestige, the English nation
decided that it could not compete in an armaments race
with America with any hope of success and that Canada
could not be defended in case of war. Hence it seemed
wiser in English eyes to foster the solidarity of the
English-speaking peoples and to place America in
England's debt by the sacrifice of England's former
ally, Japan. Despite the friction caused by the question
of the liquidation of war debts, England has never
wavered in its determination to remain on good terms
with the United States. The Dominions, with Canada
and Australia at their head, were only too glad to follow
the lead of the mother country in this matter.

While Anglo-American relations have pursued an
even course since the War, Anglo-French relations have
been subject to alternations of popular feeling. In this
case, again, England has broken with its past. In the
old days it seemed to England obvious that its policy
should be directed against the strongest of the Continental Great Powers. While, however, England had
regarded it as necessary to protect itself against Philip II,
Louis XIV, Napoleon I, and Wilhelm II, it has never
been afraid of post-War France. Even when they were

disarmed the English felt themselves superior to the French. Hence England was content to let its French friend play the part of policeman to Europe for as long as it would ensure peace and guard England's European flank. France, nevertheless, failed to carry out the task that England had prescribed for it. Instead it kept those committed to its charge in a continual state of ferment. Moreover, France did not disarm, even after England had guaranteed the Rhine frontier at Locarno. Although England was fascinated by the oratorical gifts of a Briand, it nevertheless began to ask itself whether France was really the predestined peacemaker of Europe. The cooler England's friendship for France became, the warmer grew its sympathy for the Germany of Strese-mann and Brüning. Moreover, England's growing friendship towards Germany emanated from the broad masses of the people, and especially from the Socialists and Liberals, rather than from Conservative circles. Despite their disappointment with the course followed by French policy in Europe, these circles still clung to their pro-French attitude, and were determined to act as intermediaries between France and Germany. France, however, made the pace. If the French refused their assent for any proposal, England invariably came round to the French point of view. Hence, notwithstanding the existence of much goodwill, England's friendship for Germany remained platonic and the smile froze on the face of England as soon as Germany began to raise subjects for discussion that were unpopular in France. This was the time to which England now refers as the era of missed opportunities.

While the National Socialist Revolution strengthened

the bonds uniting England to France, England now
realized to its surprise that Germany was growing
stronger, while internal political and economic disorders
were steadily sapping French vitality. It soon began to
appear as if France, where government followed
government in a swift and shadow-like succession, were
heading for revolution. A new problem was thus
created for England, where the advocates of an isola-
tionist policy became more insistent in their demand
that English policy should be kept free of European—
and thus French—entanglements. It was reserved for
Laval and the sanctions crisis to put Anglo-French
friendship to the severest test that it has undergone in
post-War years. The esteem in which France was held in
England evaporated into thin air; especially among the
masses of the people, who were solidly in favour of the
Negus and the League of Nations. The English Government, nevertheless, did not abandon its French friend
and even offered it a new Locarno in the London
Conference that followed upon the German occupation
of the Rhineland. In order to make this durable it was
necessary that the French should overcome their own
internal difficulties. The most active pro-French propaganda in England could not have won over the
nation for a policy of enduring friendship with France
if that country was in a state of dissolution or showed
signs of becoming Communist. Hence the English
Government heaved a sigh of relief when Léon Blum
put an end to Party strife and France seemed to be
stopping in its downward course. Whatever the future
might bring, France at any rate for the present continued
to be a possible ally. The summer of 1936 was to show

how close were Anglo-French relations. When the Spanish Civil War broke out and threatened to involve Europe in its maelstrom, France and England stood firmly shoulder to shoulder, as they have done ever since.

Although both France and England carefully avoid any mention of an alliance, or even an *entente*, their silence says more on the subject than floods of oratory. In reality, the threads binding the two countries together that had worked loose since the end of the War have been tightened up again. Mr. Baldwin's statement that England's frontier was the Rhine triumphed over all petty squabbles and differences of opinion. Notwithstanding the opposition of the isolationists, England was prepared on that account to enter into an alliance. Instead of withdrawing from the Continent, England once again bound itself to it during the year 1936, even if only in the form of mutual co-operation with France and Belgium—a development that was all the more remarkable since even now the broad masses of the English populace do not like France. The marriage between John Bull and Marianne is not a love match but, on the contrary, a classic example of the marriage of convenience contracted for practical reasons. England believes that its political and military interests demand that it should be France's ally. Originally this view was only held by a group of persons who derived their ideas from the Foreign Office and the War Office. But it is almost of necessity spreading to the rest of the nation. Although the English may not feel any special love for the French, the bonds of common interest are stronger than racial antipathy.

Moreover, England looks upon the British Commonwealth, the United States, and France as a great democratic *bloc* which rejects as false the notion that the only
choice confronting the world to-day is that between
Fascism and Communism. The financial support given
by England and America to France was from this
point of view a symbol of the community of interests of
world democracy.

It is idle to ask how long Franco-English friendship
will persist in these rapidly changing days. For the
present it suffices to say that during the weary post-War
years England travelled from Paris to Paris. Once
again, as formerly in Sir Edward Grey's time, the English
and French General Staffs are conferring together while
an English Secretary of State for War talks about the
Entente in Paris. Once again Germany is responsible for
the friendship between its two western neighbours.
True, since the conclusion of the Anglo-German Naval
Pact, England no longer looks balefully at the German
Fleet, of which the growth in former days was one
—though not the only—cause of the World War.
England entered the World War because it feared
that a German victory would increase the strength of
Germany to such a degree that English policy would no
longer enjoy the same freedom of choice that it had
hitherto done. English statesmen believed that it was
necessary to take measures betimes to avert the
possibility that London might one day be obliged to
dance to Berlin's piping. A load fell from their minds
when the German invasion of Belgium gave them a
moral ground for summoning the English people to
arms. In spite of the agreements between the leaders of

the Entente, England was not so firmly bound by the wording of the treaties that Parliament could not have avoided war. The first few days of August, 1914, were not unjustifiably numbered among the most anxious days ever experienced by French statesmen.

Despite many differences, the situation of Germany to-day resembles its pre-War situation in certain respects. Although England is convinced that Germany harbours no offensive intentions against the British Empire, it once again fears that Germany may achieve an increase of power as a result of a war that would endanger England's freedom in the future. Anglo-German relations to-day are dominated by military considerations. England rejects the Fascist State and the Fascist ordering of society. The Churches in England are shocked at the religious tension in Germany. All these circumstances are, nevertheless, secondary in importance to England's suspicion of Germany's revived military strength. To-day this is the chief preoccupation of and the main problem confronting English policy. England has long since recognized that Germany's domestic concerns are its own affair and nobody else's. Though anti-Fascists of the Socialist and Liberal Parties may not have a good word to say for the new Germany, the English people have not watched the revival of Germany without admiration. The English have never refused recognition for great achievements. Hence National Socialist Germany does not want for friends in England, and if a vote were to be taken as between France and Germany on grounds purely of sympathy, it is not at all certain that the latter would not gain the majority. Too many English visitors to Germany have told of German youth, German social work, German organization, and the inflexible determination with which the German people are building up a new social and political order. If it were not for the universal fear of war, and such matters as the problem of colonies and the difference between the attitudes of the two countries to Soviet Russia, there would certainly be no delay in the achievement of an Anglo-German reconciliation.

A sincere reconciliation between England and Germany would be a reconciliation between two strong nations with equal rights, and therefore wholly different from the patronizing treatment accorded by England to democratic Germany. When Germany left the Disarmament Conference and the League of Nations in 1933, the English people realized that a new day had dawned in European politics. They recognized that Germany's action marked the end of the post-War period, and that in future England would have to reckon with a Germany that had regained its self-confidence. The formula "equality of rights" had become a hard and solid fact that exercised an influence over English policy even during the critical days that saw Germany re-occupy the Rhineland. Even if German methods were criticized, the English people sympathized in principle with the German people's determination to be masters on their own soil. The moment Germany had re-organized itself and spoke again with a united voice England looked upon it once more as a Great Power that was entitled to be treated as such. Henceforth it could no longer be felt as a matter of course that the fate of a nation of sixty millions should be decided in the capitals of other countries.

Moreover, as long as the development of Germany proceeded on peaceful lines, England was glad to see a strong, healthy nation in the heart of Europe again. Although the new Germany caused England much embarrassment in foreign policy, and although many aspects of National Socialism were regarded by English eyes with dislike, England, nevertheless, also saw the National Socialist Revolution as a healing process which in some way would restore to Europe its normal aspect. The danger of a break-up of Germany that had at one time been deemed possible was now averted and with it that of the Balkanization of Central Europe. Its place was taken, however, by the problem of how to fit the new Germany into post-War Europe by means either of a new Locarno or an armaments agreement or a return of Germany to Geneva or some other arrangement. The solution of this problem has become the chief aim of English policy to-day. England seeks to prevent the isolation of Germany and must at least up to the present be regarded as free from any intention of encircling Germany.

By the time Hitler entered the Wilhelmstrasse England had long since become reconciled to the presence of Mussolini. The man who had created a new Italy, and a new type of Italian, had ceased to be the object of English criticism. England, true to its traditions, believed that it could live with Italy in peace and amity; a relationship that seemed all the easier of attainment because the two peoples had not been estranged by a war and because Fascism had not given birth to any racial or religious problems. Even in the Danubian Question England was on the side of the Duce, although it might possibly have regarded a peaceful union between Germany and Austria as the best solution. Nothing seemed to stand in the way of a lasting friendship between London and Rome, when suddenly Mussolini stretched forth his hand to seize Abyssinia. The history of the Abyssinian Question proves that the English protest against Italy's action was not inspired by imperialistic motives. Doubtless it was a severe blow to England to see a European Great Power establish itself on the shores of the Red Sea and Lake Tsana. Moreover, who could deny that the conquest of Abyssinia might be regarded in Rome as the first step towards the re-establishment of the Roman Empire? Nevertheless, England was honest in saying that it was not as a world empire but as a member of the League of Nations that it addressed its protest to Italy. Moreover, the moment the League of Nations was beaten England also retired from the struggle in order to be free to adapt its policy to the new situation. In other words—to regain its old friendship with Italy. A "gentleman's agreement" with Rome ended the Abyssinian interlude. Although it is not yet possible to visualize all the complications to which the Spanish Civil War may give rise, Mussolini's confirmation of the territorial *status quo* in the Mediterranean has calmed England's worst fears. If it were not for the existence of the Spanish problem, everything would point to the continuance of the Anglo-Italian reconciliation. Both nations are ready to forget the quarrel caused by Abyssinia between two old friends.

Nevertheless, even if the historic friendship is re-established, the days are past when England considered it as "unthinkable" that Italy should be numbered among its enemies. England cannot forget that a Great Power, strong with the strength of youth, may one day, from the Red Sea and Sicily, lay a hand upon the main artery of the British Empire—the Mediterranean route to India. No matter how cordial relations may become between London and Rome, England will have to be on its guard. Too much is at stake for England to rely solely upon friendship between the nations. Hence England is at work consolidating its relations with the other Mediterranean countries. In the same way as France was useful on the Rhine, it has proved to be England's natural ally in the Mediterranean. While no formal alliance was concluded between France and England, the necessity of avoiding publicity was not present in the case of Anglo-Egyptian relations. The long-wished-for treaty with Egypt, which was concluded after the Abyssinian War, compensated England on the Lower Nile for what it had lost at its sources. British diplomacy made masterly use of Egypt's fear of Italian aggression. It was only logical that England should follow up its treaty with Egypt by securing its relations with Greece, Yugoslavia, and Turkey, as well as by abandoning its former veto on the opening of the Straits of the Bosphorus and the Dardanelles. Russia thus saw the path to the Mediterranean opened before it. In its pursuit of diplomatic security England did not lose sight of military safeguards. The Rome Agreement did not restrict the right of England to fortify Malta and Cyprus, from whence, as also from the coast of Palestine, England can at least partially protect the eastern Mediterranean from attack : a system of defence which was made more complete by the establishment of an air route across Irak to the Persian Gulf—an aerial parallel to the sea-passage through the Mediterranean. Since the Mediterranean route has been endangered, South Africa has come to acquire an increased strategical importance in English eyes that has resulted in proposals for the construction on Union territory of airports and the enlargement of South African harbours. Even if the route to India by way of South Africa involves loss of time, it is better than none, especially since the Spanish Civil War has exposed England's position in the western Mediterranean to new dangers.

None of these measures stands in the way of England's working to restore its former friendship with Italy. England can only sleep in peace if Italy can be fitted into a political system which makes war in the Mediterranean impossible. In England's eyes France is a friend; Italy potentially friend or foe. To make every effort to win Italy's friendship and to protect itself against Italy's enmity is the quintessence of England's Mediterranean policy to-day, in spite of the very strong antipathy felt by the broad masses against Mussolini.

A single incident—the Abyssinian War—served to disturb the even tenor of post-War Anglo-Italian relations. England's relations with Russia also took an unexpected course, but for quite different reasons. At the close of the World War England and Russia were openly hostile to each other. Their mutual hostility continued even after England had ceased to support the White Russians and had resumed diplomatic relations with Moscow. England felt the Soviet hand in India and China, and even within its own island frontiers. The

Zinovieff Letter, which has never been quite satisfac-
torily explained, sufficed to overthrow a Socialist
Government in England, while the Arcos scandal nearly
brought the relations between the two countries to
breaking-point. The German Republic was blamed
for sitting at the same table with the common enemy of
humanity. Soviet Russia was not slow in repaying its
enemies in their own coin. A caricature of Sir Austen
Chamberlain was publicly displayed at every workers'
demonstration in Moscow in those days.

At the same time advocates were not wanting for the
cause of Anglo-Russian *rapprochement*. Although English
Socialists rejected Communism, they never lost interest
in the Soviet attempt to build up a modern state upon
non-capitalist foundations. Moreover, English capitalism
saw no reason why it should not make money by
trading with proletarian Russia. America had already
resumed trade relations with the Soviet State. Prophecies
of the imminent collapse of the Soviet Government had
also proved false, and therefore if England really wished
to arrive at an understanding with Russia, it was bound
to accept the fact of the continued existence of the Soviet
rule. The decisive turn in Anglo-Russian relations did
not come, however, until the Soviet Government
expressed its willingness to join the League of Nations.
In this fashion Russia threw a bridge across to the
English Conservatives that only became firmer when
France, the historic friend of Russia, had also found its
way back to the Kremlin. England raised no objection
to the new Franco-Russian alliance. When, moreover,
England's economic situation improved, when India
calmed down in an astonishing manner, and when

Communism failed to make any headway in China, England began to believe that it was immune to the virus of Bolshevism. Indeed, there were numbers of English people who hoped that the inclusion of the Soviet Republic in the European family of nations meant that Bolshevism was becoming bourgeois and nationalist, and who had visions of the fulfilment of this hope when the Trotskyists were crushed. The paler the Communist spectre became in English eyes, the greater became the military and political significance of Moscow for the British Empire. The Soviet Republic lay between Germany and Japan—two states that aroused deep anxiety in the minds of English statesmen. It is true that the die-hard Tories in England uttered warnings against wolves in sheep's clothing. Nevertheless, the Left was wholly in favour of friendship with Russia, while the Conservatives approved of the resumption of normal relations : a resumption upon which the seal was soon afterwards set by the grant of a large financial credit to Russia. If France had succumbed to Bolshevism there can be no doubt that England would again have changed its policy. Since, however, the Blum Government succeeded in maintaining itself so long in office, the growing intimacy of England and Russia has hardly been interfered with, even by the Spanish Civil War and despite England's obvious anxiety to prevent Communism from spreading to Africa and the Mediter-ranean. While it is impossible to foretell how events will develop in this storm centre of Europe, and therefore what will be the character of Anglo-Russian relations in the future, it may suffice to state here that for the moment relations between London and Moscow are becoming progressively more friendly. For this reason England refuses to enter any anti-Communist *bloc* and is not prepared to sacrifice its good relations with Moscow for the sake of friendship with Germany. Such, at all events, was the position at the beginning of the year 1937, when Soviet Russia forms the strongest obstacle in the path of Anglo-German *rapprochement*.

If Germany is one of the two chief reasons for Anglo-Russian friendship, the other is Japan. England looked on with disapproval at Japan's invasion of Manchukuo and feared the consequent threat to the "Open Door" in China which is so important to English merchants and investors. It is with even greater anxiety that England regards the strategical centre of its military power in the Far East—Singapore—whose defences were neglected in recent years. If England should become involved in a European war, and if Japan were to take advantage of England's preoccupation to undertake a *coup de main* at Singapore, England would be cut off from China and Australia. Until Singapore has been so strongly fortified that it could withstand a siege and could serve as England's naval base in the Far East, it forms a serious breach in the English defence system, which is not filled in even by England's friendship with the United States. Though England's situation is improving with every month that is gained, several years will probably have to be spent in feverishly fortifying Singapore before the Japanese spectre is finally laid. Moreover, the English Navy must be strengthened if it is to be able to defend England's Far Eastern possessions. Meanwhile nothing remains for England but to cultivate good relations with Japan, and simultaneously to consolidate its friendship with the United States and Russia as possible allies in event of a war with Japan. Added to these possible allies by reasons of propinquity is Holland, which has recently become one of England's closest friends. As in Europe, so in the East, military preparations run parallel to political; just as to a certain degree England places Germany on a par with Japan as a possible rival. There is, it is true, one considerable difference between them; England no longer as in pre-War days fears Germany's economic competition. Japan, on the other hand, which undercuts English prices despite protective tariffs, has become England's most dangerous rival in the markets of the world. England's textile manufacturers in Lancashire have much to say on this subject.

The firing of the first shot in Europe or the Far East will mark the failure of England's policy, the chief aim of which has been the prevention of war. In order to preserve peace England has entered into two military alliances in Europe, one with France, the other with Belgium. For the rest, especially in regard to Eastern Europe, England has left itself free to choose between neutrality or belligerency according to the merits of each case. Nevertheless, England has certainly not declared itself disinterested in Eastern Europe. Czechoslovakia, in particular, is causing anxiety. The circumstances in which a war was declared would nevertheless be of the utmost importance in influencing England's decision. For again, as in the case of Belgium, the British Government would need a moral slogan to rouse its people. Up to a certain point England can make use of the League of Nations for this purpose, and in any case it is unlikely to take up arms in a cause which is not that of the League itself. Geneva not only adds to the number of foreign allies and is useful for moral purposes; it also provides a means of applying pressure to the Dominions as members of the League to join in the war. If it is in any way possible, England is likely to wage any future war under the banner of the League of Nations : a fact that explains the dual significance that the League of Nations has for England. It is in the first place an institution for preventing war, and in the second —if it has failed in its first duty—it is the focal point of offensive alliances that also include those of England with the Dominions.

For this reason England clings to the League of Nations despite all disappointments. But not necessarily to the League of Nations in its present form. England is by no means averse to a reform of the League and of the system of collective security. In this connection the formation of regional pacts is of importance. These pacts resemble the agreements by which England has bound itself to aid in the defence of France and Belgium. England is at last beginning to realize that the League of Nations has no future merely as an institution for the preservation of the *status quo*. How precisely the required machinery for revision and arbitration is to be brought into existence remains a mystery for the present. To-day the question which is agitating English minds is how a German nation that is growing in numbers and strength is to be given the freedom of movement necessary for its future development. Since Japan and Italy have secured space for expansion by means of war, it seems unfair to the average English-man that Germany, which has not taken up arms, should go empty. From the days of Sir Samuel Hoare the British Government has repeatedly declared itself to be ready to discuss the problem of raw materials. Although the Tories object to its discussion, the question of mandates also remains unsolved. The Left Parties in England are specially alive to the responsibility which England has assumed in Ottawa by shutting off so large a part of the world within tariff walls. It is these Parties that are willing to compensate other countries for the results of the Ottawa policy by placing the colonial possessions of the Powers in some form or other under the control of the League of Nations in order that these territories may thereby be accessible to all the states that are members of the League. For the present this must remain a Utopian ideal. Another scheme, therefore, seems to be gaining support: the plan of establishing international colonial companies or associations. It is believed that an invitation to Germany to join such chartered companies would give it an opportunity of sharing in the exploitation of colonial territories. English opposition to the return to Germany of her former colonies remains astonishingly strong. Moreover, it has not lessened as a result of the strategic considerations raised by rearmament. England fears lest Germany might make use of West Africa to establish submarine and air bases that would endanger England's lines of communication with South Africa. Although England is fully alive to the contribution that would be made by a settlement of the colonial question to the cause of peace, it must also not be forgotten that the British lion is not in the habit of voluntarily surrendering its prey. As a result of England's study of the problem of

Germany's need for colonies and raw materials, only two fundamental conclusions have so far been reached: first, that to throw small pieces of colonial territory to Germany would serve no useful purpose, but would be like a drop of water on a hot stone and would be useless to Germany itself in the long run; second, that the questions of raw materials and colonies form only a part of a general political, military, and economic settlement in the course of which Germany would have to be induced to resume its membership of the League of Nations.

The return of Germany to the League of Nations is the aim that England has set before itself ever since Germany turned its back upon Geneva. England may conclude treaties with France, and coquet with Russia, but it will only regard the peace of Europe as assured when Germany has in some form or other been reincorporated in a European system of peace. Three possibilities alone confront England to-day: to formulate its policy either with, without, or against Germany. While England does not exclude the second and third possibilities from its calculations, it would prefer the first. England would certainly regard a failure to achieve an understanding with Germany as a heavy defeat for its policy. It nevertheless remains an open question what contribution England is prepared to make towards such an understanding, and when it will make it. England must have realized by now that words are of no use to Germany and that deeds are necessary to put an end to a state of things that threatens Germany's life and liberty. England taxes its rich citizens mercilessly in order to provide its poor with a means of subsistence fit for human beings. Can England not realize that wealthy nations can only live in peace if they make some sacrifice for the sake of those peoples with whom Fate has dealt harshly? The future of the world may depend upon whether an instrument of justice and equity can be created in international affairs similar to the social services of the nations. Can England not realize that its responsibility is the greater because it is the richest among the nations? The answer to this question will show whether England's love of peace is anything more than the insurance policy with which a rich man protects himself against the loss of his wealth.

Whatever the future may bring forth, Anglo-German relations are at present in the balance. The slow progress made by the negotiations for an Anglo-German understanding is the more regrettable because, despite the acute differences between National Socialism and English Democracy, the post-War years have led to a cultural *rapprochement* between the two nations. Strange as it may sound, England is more German and Germany more English than before the World War. Germany has learnt from England that knowledge alone does not bring happiness and that it made a mistake in neglecting the moral and physical development of its people for the sake of book-learning. The German educational ideal is no longer a spectacled book-worm, but a morally and physically sound youth unafraid of responsibility. This is just as English in character as is the value laid by modern German education upon training for leadership. On the other hand, England has learnt something from the German Youth Movement and the *Wandervögel*, just as its social conscience was strengthened by German progress in a sphere in which England—as in many other cases—took Germany as its model. Moreover, the intellectual, artistic, and scientific interests that are playing an increasingly large part in English life have caused English and German ways of living to resemble one another more closely than hitherto. London to-day is as much a musical and theatrical centre as Berlin, with which it was not to be compared a few decades ago, while medicine and chemistry, which were formerly almost a German monopoly, are coming to be more and more at home in England. The period of England's political and military weakness was one of steady progress in English intellectual life—a fact that gives the lie to the old saying that the English are a "nation of shopkeepers." A new generation is growing up in the British Isles whose understanding of the educational ideals that have made Germany great is steadily increasing. While Germany has opened its windows and let fresh air in upon the stuffiness of academic pedantry, the youth of England has been devoting an increasing amount of its time to study in libraries, places of popular education, and laboratories. It should surely not be impossible for these generations in Germany and England to establish between them a peace that was denied to their fathers.

War or peace is in England's eyes the great problem of the future. Even if peace were to be preserved, England would still have its anxieties. Before the War Ireland was the Achilles' heel of the British Empire. To-day it would only be a source of danger were the Irish Free State to attempt to seize Ulster. The secession of the Irish Free State from the Commonwealth would not of itself endanger its peace or stability. England, for its part, is willing to allow the Free State to follow its own path, provided only that it does not attack Ulster or permit itself to be used by foreign Powers as a military or naval base. For this latter reason alone England will insist upon receiving military guarantees from the Free State. At the same time the advantages that England, which buys ninety per cent. of the Free State's products, can offer to the Free State in an economic sense are so great that there should be no difficulty about concluding a settlement of the dispute between them on this basis. It was for this reason that De Valera yielded only to the demands of his own extremists to the extent of abolishing the post of Governor-General and thereby doing away with the personal representation of the King in the Free State. His action also restricted England's opportunities of keeping an eye upon the Free State's internal affairs. On the other hand, De Valera shrank from proclaiming the Free State's secession from the Commonwealth, which would have had for its consequences the Free State's exclusion from the British tariff system and the threat to Irish workers in England of a withdrawal of the permission to work on the ground that they had now become foreigners. Despite his passionate devotion to the ideal of a free and independent Ireland, De Valera has shown that he also recognizes the benefits which Ireland has received from its membership of the British Commonwealth of Nations. Moreover, even if the extremists in Ireland were to have their way and proclaim an independent republic, it would still be possible for Republican Ireland and England to conclude an alliance based on a community of interests, after the pattern of the Anglo-Egyptian treaty. Whether or not the Free State remains within the Commonwealth is, however, of less importance than whether or not it insists upon the inclusion of Ulster within an united Ireland ; and that in its turn depends upon whether Southern Ireland can continue to exist without Belfast's industry. Apart from these questions, it would seem that the quarrels that have divided Ireland and England for centuries are on the way to a settlement. Although England is prepared for surprises, it nevertheless no longer looks upon Ireland as being—or at any rate as likely to be in the future—a running sore upon the body politic of the Commonwealth.

On the other hand, despite the fact that calm has succeeded the uproar of the Gandhi-Irwin period, England's eyes are steadfastly fixed upon India: for there a gigantic experiment is being made. England is engaged in India on a task that is perhaps the greatest known to modern history. If England had taken it upon itself to work out a constitution for Europe, it would have been no more daring an attempt than that of seeking to weld together the three hundred and forty million inhabitants of India into a nation. India is not a state that is simultaneously a racial entity. It is, on the contrary, a mixture of races and colours from the darkest black to the fairest of the fair, of religions from the refined spirituality of Buddhism to the lowest forms of idolatry, of mediæval despotism and modern government, of dialects, languages, and customs. In short—it is a land of contrasts that are far sharper and more fundamental than those to be found between the

European states. Furthermore, India is divided up into two great political divisions: the feudal native states with a population of eighty millions; and British India, that is to say, the Indian provinces, with a population of two hundred and sixty millions. England's relations to the native states and British India are of a fundamentally different nature. While England rules British India more or less as it rules a colony, the Maharajahs are very largely rulers of their own lands. Their relations to England are regulated by means of treaties, in which the Maharajahs abandon their right to an independent foreign policy and in return are free to rule their territories at their own discretion upon the sole condition that their rule does not lead to economic distress and political unrest. England only interferes in the Native States when it deems its own interests to be seriously endangered or in the increasingly rare instances of a Maharajah's misrule. It was not therefore easy for the Maharajahs at the Round Table Conference in London to declare themselves willing to enter an Indian Federation, even if their treaty rights were reserved to them. For India itself this was an event of enormous importance. For the first time since the days of the Mogul Empire the opportunity has been given to the peoples of India to act together as a single nation.

The constitution that has been given to this vast agglomeration of native states and provinces bears the impress of western Democracy. It remains to be seen whether western democratic notions will take root and flourish in India's soil. Once Federalism is instituted, the Viceroy, as personal representative of the King-Emperor, is to form an Indian Government from the members of two elective chambers composed of representatives both of British India and of the Native States. The democratization of the Central Government is exceeded in extent by that of the provincial governments, that are subject to the control of a Governor and an elective provincial assembly. While provincial autonomy has already begun to work, the Federal constitution has not yet been put into practice. This provincial autonomy is the means by which the English Government seeks to educate the Indian masses up to the task of self-government. Until such time as India is ready to take the reins of government wholly into its own hands England retains for itself guarantees of a military, financial, and police nature. England's purpose in retaining these powers in its own hands is in reality that of making as little use of them as possible and only employing them when law and order or Anglo-Indian trade are threatened by disturbance. The fitter the Indians show themselves to use the constitution that has been given to them, the less will England interfere in Indian affairs. Stage by stage and guided by the ancient principle *solvitur ambulando*, England is seeking to educate India up to being a self-governing Dominion. It is, however, over this very question that Indian and English opinion are at variance. As was only to be expected, Indian opinion regards the safeguards imposed by England in granting the constitution as so many chains with which England seeks to bind India to the Commonwealth. Hence it was a severe disappointment to Indian opinion that the new constitution did not even accord to India the full Dominion status that was the least that the Indian peoples expected to receive. In this

connection the existence of a question that England dislikes discussing may be mentioned: Does the Statute of
Westminster confer the right of secession from the
Commonwealth upon the Dominions? As far as India
is concerned the question is at present merely of
academic interest: for India to-day enjoys only a semi—
at the most three-quarter—Dominion status.

The immediate question confronting the British
Government is whether the peoples of India can be
induced to co-operate in the government and parliamentary life of their country and to what extent they
are capable of such co-operation. Will the Indians boy-
cott the new constitution and thereby reduce it to an
absurdity, or will sufficient of them participate in its
working to preserve at least an appearance of democracy? Furthermore, the question that still awaits an
answer is whether democracy in India is practicable.
If it is not, what form of government is suited to the
Indian temperament? The weakest point in the programme of the Congress Party and other fighters for
India's independence is the fact that they have never
returned any answer to this question or to England's
repeated demands for alternative proposals. It is only
necessary in this connection to recall the differences that
exist in India between Hindus and Mohammedans, rich
and poor, princes and nationalist politicians, in order to
realize that England can easily postpone the solution of
the problem that is desired by Indian nationalist patriots
merely by making skilful use of these differences.
England answers their arguments by saying that if
it were to remove its protecting hand India would
become the prey of internal dissensions and, perhaps,

fall a victim to Bolshevism. Nevertheless, it is inevitable that the desire for freedom should grow steadily stronger in politically-minded Indians, and that even the Dominion status which India is now seeking to achieve would not be the final stage in political development. If England were to be involved in war, India would immediately become a source of great danger: for it will not permit another opportunity like the World War to pass away without making some endeavour to break its chains. At all events, England will certainly have need of all its statesmanship and diplomacy if Indian self-government is not to lead to separatism. The history of recent years nevertheless contains a warning for those who think that India is already lost. During Lord Willingdon's viceroyalty the relations between India and England not only did not grow worse but actually improved to a surprising degree. The Congress movement under Gandhi's leadership has—at least temporarily—lost much of its importance. "At least temporarily"—because India is incalculable. The movement for independence, for example, may drag along slowly for generations, or it may suddenly recover its original impetus. One thing alone is certain—India must continually be a source of anxiety to England in the future as in the past. Of all the fissures in the structure of the British Empire that on the Ganges is certainly the most dangerous.

Moreover, the rest of the Empire is not immune from danger. Even as the Indian masses have aroused themselves to political activity, so the black races in Africa may one day weary of white rule. The Union of South Africa is fully alive to this menace. The vast extent of the

British Empire also makes it impossible to foretell where trouble will break out at any time. Its rulers must be prepared for any and every emergency and must never lose sight of the whole in their momentary pre-occupation with a part. For this reason alone the British ship of state must be navigated with extreme caution and at a slow speed.

The vast size of the Empire is also responsible for the fact that England trains the different portions for self-government. England itself has not enough men available for the administration of the whole Empire, and is therefore compelled to rely upon the man on the spot. The Englishman's task is, nevertheless, rendered easier in this respect by the fact that self-government is one of the greatest of his political ideals. For its sake England is willing to take the risk that self-government may one day function so perfectly that its own sons will no longer be wanted in its overseas territories. It is in this sense that the British Empire resembles a company organized for business purposes from which the partners are individually free to withdraw if the returns do not correspond with their expectations. England must therefore be constantly on the watch to see that membership of the Commonwealth is made worth the while of the individual states composing it. For this purpose it is essential that the motherland should remain strong and healthy as well as possessing a clever and skilfully directed policy. The old saying that it is easier for a mother to support seven sons than seven sons a mother may be applied with some exactitude to the relations between England and its overseas territories. The Dominions are already too independent and too conscious of their own powers to be willing to support the mother country if any weakening of its vitality should one day make such a course necessary. Only an economically prosperous and politically healthy England, strong enough to resist pressure from outside, can be the real pivot of a world empire.

The future of the British Empire therefore depends upon England itself. It has already been pointed out above how England overcame its economic difficulties and how it is hard at work to make good the deficiency in its defences. England was able to do this because the English people in the hour of need were wise enough to elect a strong and non-Party Government. Nevertheless, it would be a mistake to think that all internal difficulties have thereby been overcome, or even diminished in their extent. These difficulties cannot be overcome while the English people are sharply divided into two classes by economic conditions. One class leads a more carefree, luxurious, and interesting life than is to be found anywhere else in Europe, while the poorer class has to content itself with relatively little. Despite the fact that much has been done to better social conditions, the standard of living in England is set by the wealthy classes. England is indeed a joyless country for the poor. It lacks both the far-reaching organization of leisure that is to be found in Germany and the cafés that enliven the evenings of the poorer classes in France. Moreover, the poorer classes in England live less comfortably and fare far worse in regard to food than the similar classes across the Channel. If it is also remembered that the climate is depressing, that cheap and easily accessible health resorts are few in number, that people are crowded together in great cities, and that the average Englishman is lacking in intellectual interests and pursuits, it is hardly too much to say that persons possessed of incomes below a certain level live better on the "poverty-stricken" Continent than they do in "wealthy" England. At the same time these disadvantages are compensated for to some extent by the greater possibilities of advancement that England offers to a clever and hard-working man. Moreover, it is also necessary to remember that virtually no restrictions are placed in England upon political liberty.

The glaring contrast between rich and poor in England is more strongly reflected in the composition of the political Parties to-day than ever before in its history. For political life in England has undergone a fundamental change in recent years. For centuries England has been governed alternately by two Parties, formerly known as Whigs and Tories and latterly as Liberals and Conservatives. Notwithstanding the sharp differences between these two Parties, neither sought to make any fundamental change in the political and social order in the country. It was reserved for a new third Party—the Labour Party—to attack the foundations of English social and political life. The three-party system nevertheless did not prove satisfactory, and the partial absorption of the Liberal Party by the other two Parties would have been wholly welcome if it had not brought a new danger in its train. If the Liberals either wholly disappear or are reduced to impotence in the future, it is inevitable in accordance with democratic principles that the Opposition will achieve power one day, and therefore that England must reckon with the possibility—indeed the certainty—of a Socialist Government. With the disappearance of the Liberals there would be no other alternative. It is true that since the War England has already had two Socialist Governments. Since, however, the Labour Government did not possess an absolute majority on either occasion and was dependent for its existence upon the Liberal vote, it was forced to proceed cautiously. The question to-day is what a Labour Government would do if it were wholly independent of middle-class support. The day on which a purely Socialist Government takes office will be a fateful day in English history. Up to the present the Socialists have only been successful in obtaining absolute majorities in certain municipalities.

Nevertheless, it is necessary to bear in mind the peculiar character of the English Labour Party. With the exception of a numerically small Left Wing, it is free from Marxian doctrinaires. The English workman has never allowed his head to be turned by abstract economic theories. Notwithstanding the efforts of agitators and propagandists, the sound, practical common sense of the English people has always rejected nebulous theories. The English working man is fully alive to the fact that a Socialist state does not spring into being overnight. Hence he is content to proceed stage by stage as long as the standard of living of the working classes is raised and an end is made to glaring differences in income. Out of this desire there was born the famous "Budget Socialism" that has pressed so hard upon the wealthy classes. The death duties on an estate of two millions total one million, and on an estate of one million amount to forty per cent. Sooner or later the idle rich are therefore bound to disappear. Moreover, it is obvious that a Socialist Government commanding an absolute majority in the House of Commons will not be content with such half-measures. The programme of the Labour Party contains such demands as the nationalization of the banks, mines, and key industries as well as the provision of work or, alternatively, bread for the working population. The burning question is therefore whether an omnipotent Labour Government will be able to carry through its reforms in such a manner that the enormously complex economic and industrial structure of England does not suffer collapse and bring about the impoverishment of the disappointed masses, who in their despair might take to revolution. What would also be the effect upon the Dominions of a financial and industrial collapse of the mother country? What would be the reaction of India to any—even temporary—weakening of England? Furthermore, it is necessary to ask what degree of unity is likely to be achieved within a Socialist Government itself. If it is remembered what very various and divergent elements are comprised within the Labour movement, the question seems at least fair and pertinent. Even between the more or less conservative Trade Unions and the political Labour Party there exist sharp differences of opinion, while the extreme Left is hardly distinguishable from Communism. The fact that Communism is so weak in England to-day and that the Centre and Right Wings of the Party reject the idea of a common Labour Front does not constitute a guarantee that a movement towards the Left will not take place in the future. Up to the present the working-classes have not been able to produce a personality sufficiently commanding to be able to unite all the various Labour groups beneath a single banner.

The English Socialists are therefore in a state of ferment of which the outcome cannot as yet be predicted. The Party has indeed time in which to consolidate itself. The Conservatives with their Liberal and National Labour supporters seem to be so firmly fixed in the saddle that it would be a miracle if the next elections—in any case they are not due for four years—were to bring about any startling change. Although it is never safe to prophesy in politics, and especially English politics, it is hardly likely that there will be a Socialist Government for the next eight or ten years. It is possible that by that time the Left Wing workers and intellectuals will have formed a separate Party, and that the Liberals will have joined the remainder of the Labour Party in working out a programme capable of being carried through without serious upheavals. Whatever title England's political Parties may adopt, England has always been able in the hour of need to count upon the support of the anonymous Party of Sound Common Sense. It is because England trusts to the common sense of its people that it regards Communism as too foreign for English consumption.

In order to prevent the radicalization of the masses the National Government has made great efforts to alleviate social evils. A serious endeavour has at last been made to do away with the notorious slum districts, that are a disgrace to England, and at the same time to solve the even more difficult problem of overcrowding.

The building of one-family houses living in which tends to change the English working classes more and more into lower middle class, is being speeded up. The greatest anxiety of all, however, is at present being caused by the three distressed areas of South Wales, Cumberland, and the North-East coast, where want and hopelessness are the greater since the permanent loss of their markets makes any reconstruction on the old basis impossible. For this reason a million and a half workers belonging for the most part to the mining and textile industries, the latter of which has been seriously hit by Japanese competition, are condemned to idleness at a time when England is beginning to show signs of renewed economic prosperity. The task confronting England is therefore to plan a more equitable division of this renewed prosperity. It is for this reason that the Government makes great efforts to help the distressed areas by the establishment of new industries—armament factories among others—in order that these districts may at least share to some degree in the general economic revival. The alternative in the form of the transportation of the work-people from the distressed areas into the districts that are experiencing the economic revival has proved impracticable.

Emigration across the ocean seems to be as difficult to organize as emigration from one county to another. The overseas parts of the Empire cannot make use of either elderly unemployed persons or of unskilled labourers. They demand skilled workers or strong young farmers and their wives. Unfortunately the type required by the Dominions and Colonies is the very type that England cannot produce. England therefore sees the time coming in which the Dominions will recruit their man-power from non-English countries, and especially from Germany. England would welcome such a course in so far it would mean some relief for the pressure of population in Germany and thus aid in the pacification of Europe. On the other hand, England fears that a large number of foreign immigrants might cause the foreign element within the Empire to become dangerously large. England is therefore beginning seriously to consider the secondary problems, both quantitative and qualitative, that are involved in the general problem of the future of its population. Apart from the fact that the birth rate is low, the proportion of rural and urban population is continually changing, to the detriment of the former. It will be remembered what was said in the chapter on "Town and Country" on the subject of the disappearance of the farming class and the decay of agriculture. The question that awaits an answer is whether the Conservative Government that is likely to remain in office for years to come will be able to arrest this process. If not, then even less is to be hoped of its Socialist successor. In any event the problems of population and agriculture are bound with the progress of time to rank higher on the list of England's anxieties. It is therefore significant that England should have chosen this particular time to launch a campaign for "national fitness."

The emigration problem is not the only problem that causes England anxiety in its relations with its Dominions. The development of their own industries has meanwhile made great progress, with the result that the Dominions now produce within their own frontiers many manufactured goods which they were formerly in the habit of buying from England. Moreover, despite imperial preference, the Dominions are by no means disposed to discontinue their trade with foreign countries. Indeed, the Dominions have been proved to gain more from the Ottawa Agreement than the mother country, which is as a consequence seeking by negotiation with the Dominions to improve its own position : an object of which the attainment has been rendered more difficult by the fact that England— for reasons which have already been stated—is trying hard to rescue its agriculture and its rural population from a slough of despond, while, on the other hand, the Dominions are only prepared to buy the mother country's manufactured goods if it takes their foodstuffs and raw materials in exchange. The Imperial Conference that meets in London at the time of the Coronation will therefore be of considerable importance not only for the discussion of military and international, but also of economic problems. Everything suggests that the Empire Conference will enhance the loyalty of the Dominions, increase the strategical co-ordination of the Empire, and prepare the ground for further economic negotiations. England was clever to summon the conference immediately after the Coronation, an event that will fill every member of the vast Commonwealth with a pride only comparable to the old "civis Romanus sum."

The fact that England has recovered economically and militarily under the rule of the National Government is due to its enormous reserves and the patriotism of its people rather than to the emergence of any new

ideas. Reconstruction has been carried out in accordance
with orthodox financial and economic principles rather
than by the employment on a large scale of emergency
relief measures and compulsory organization of work.
Similarly, England has not embarked upon any reform
of its parliamentary procedure despite the fact that this
works more slowly and laboriously than the methods
employed to-day by younger and more dynamic
states. England, indeed, has hardly changed its gait
in a world that is full of abrupt changes. No fresh ideas
that might be useful to other countries have come from
the Empire to which so large a part of the world belongs.
Modern England has produced no statesman of the
intellectual fecundity of Mussolini, Hitler, Lenin, or
Roosevelt—whatever one may think of them as
individuals. England has pursued its old paths and has
admittedly progressed along them. It is, however, a
question as to whether or not the road that was worth
following yesterday and to-day will also be worth
pursuing in the future. Does not the present age, that is
England's age as much as that of any other country,
demand a more centralized type of organization than is
possible under the English system of individualistic
laisser faire? Although the English are good organizers,
their co-operative capacity is poor. If an art gallery is
being built in England, the director, the architect, and
the engineer responsible for lighting and heating will
meet for the first time at the inaugural ceremony. In
the same way town planning, which is looked upon as
an obvious necessity in Germany, is still in its infancy
in England. It took a Socialist Minister to bring order
into the chaos of London transport. It needs years of

negotiation before even the simplest co-operative societies for buying and selling can be brought into existence. While Germany is threatened with over-organization, England is exposed to-day to the danger of under-organization, that leads in its turn to friction and a waste of energy that must some day exhaust even the forces that England has at its command. Although England owes very much to the spirit of independence in its people, the day may yet come when the independence of the individual will become a danger to the common weal. Perhaps it is in this very sphere that there is the greatest need for educational work if England is not to be out-distanced in a world that is organizing itself more and more. Extensive cultivation alone is bound to lead to a diminution of resources—no matter how vast they may be.

Though England's troubles and dangers have not been minimized, and its faults have not been glossed over, it would be wrong to go to the other extreme and cry "Finis Britanniæ," because of social injustices, centres of unrest, and a want of organization. England is an immensely powerful country. English men and women are not decadent but now as formerly capable of a great future. It is not to be wondered at that there should be signs of decadence in a country that is so rich and possesses such an ancient civilization. Nevertheless, it would be mistaken to argue from the existence in its midst of a handful of decadents that the English nation as a whole is degenerate. Its ancestral virtues of tenacity, honesty, knowledge of life, and will to power are still flourishing. England may be a slow country, but it is not a tired country, any more than an adult man must be deemed to be worn out because his pace of work is different from what it was in his youth. What England may have lost in youthful momentum it has gained in experience. Thus England's power and greatness cannot be gauged by the number of its soldiers or the extent of its wealth. Its well-being is watched over by the cleverest and most adroit diplomacy in the world. England's might is not confined to its visible and immediately realizable forces. England's real battle-front is never the actual front line but the reserves which it will not draw upon until the hour of need. Just because England is careful not to waste its energies and because it is not interested in doing everything it does at high pressure, it has enormous untapped reserves of a material and moral nature. To overlook these is to make a false estimate of England. Many have lived to do penance for mistaking the Englishman's indifference and lack of ambition for weakness.

It is true that England is no longer in quite the same fortunate position as in the past. The aeroplane has made an end to its isolation from the Continent and the submarine threatens its lines of communication and sources of food supply. The strategical advantage formerly given to it by its geographical position is as much a thing of the past as the industrial predominance which made England rich. England can no longer rely upon its exceptional position, but is obliged to enter the international arena both as combatant and merchant under the same—if not, indeed, less favourable— conditions as its enemies and competitors. The future of England is likely to be more filled with difficulties than was the past; the demands made on sons and grandsons greater than those made on fathers and grandfathers. It would be rash to prophesy whether the new race that England requires will be developed. If, however, the facts alone are regarded, it must be noted that England has extricated itself from the period of military and economic inertia that followed upon the World War and also from the abdication crisis of 1936 with a vigour that does not warrant the conclusion that the nation is exhausted. On the contrary. The last few years have shown that England's will to power is still unbroken; that the Englishman is still conscious of the responsibility devolving upon him for his vast Empire; and that he is still convinced that England has a mission to fulfil in the world. It is significant that England rejects Communism as it rejects Fascism. Although a parliamentary reform that would give to the Government an increased authority is within the bounds of possibility, England now as always clings to its democratic organization of state and society. Much as they may learn from the governmental experiments of the foreigner, the English people refuse to allow any interference with the democratic foundations of England and English society.

The fact that the Englishman clings to this ideal is significant in the highest degree. Calm and far-sighted as he may be in his capacity as a business man, the Englishman's full powers do not develop until he feels the moral impulse driving him. In this sense the Englishman is an idealistic materialist. His head is not so far in the clouds that he loses sight of the earth; he does not cling so firmly to the ground that he cannot see the sky.

QUO VADIS, BRITANNIA?

He is more practical than the Teuton and more in touch with eternity than the Latin. Not only his cultural but also his spiritual position lies midway between the two. His feet are very firmly planted on this position, and never more so than when he feels himself to be threatened. No one knows the English who has not seen them in the hour of danger. At such times a national force fed from subterranean springs gushes forth that is the mightier because it is not allowed to run to waste but is guided into the proper channels by a cool intelligence. If the Goths had possessed a Narses, they might have become Englishmen instead of leaving it to history to record the tragedy of a waste of the most splendid human material. The Englishman does not waste his energies. An infallible instinct and a political wisdom handed down from ancient days keep watch and ward together over the powers of self-sacrifice and the dare-devil courage of the English race in order that these may not be squandered on useless purposes. The secret of England's rise to greatness is to be found in this mixture of strength and wisdom. Upon it is dependent how long the British Empire will be able to stay on the heights to which it has risen after centuries of struggle.

THE END

PRINTED IN GREAT BRITAIN BY WILLIAM CLOWES AND SONS, LIMITED,
LONDON AND BECCLES.